seafood kitchen

Vicki Wild

photography by Jennifer Soo

seafood

kitchen

over 100 recipes
for fish and shellfish

HarperCollins*Publishers*

HarperCollins*Publishers*

First published in Australia in 1999
by HarperCollins*Publishers* Pty Limited
ACN 009 913 517
A member of the HarperCollins*Publishers* (Australia) Pty Limited Group
http://www.harpercollins.com.au

HarperCollins*Publishers*
25 Ryde Road, Pymble, Sydney, NSW 2073, Australia
31 View Road, Glenfield, Auckland 10, New Zealand
77-85 Fulham Palace Road, London W6 8JB, United Kingdom
Hazelton Lanes, 55 Avenue Road, Suite 2900, Toronto, Ontario M5R 3L2
and 1995 Markham Road, Scarborough, Ontario M1B 5M8, Canada
10 East 53rd Street, New York NY 10022, USA

National Library of Australia Cataloguing-in-Publication data:

Wild, Vicki.
Seafood kitchen.
ISBN 0 7322 5799 9.
1. Cookery (Seafood). I. Soo, Jennifer. II. Title.
641.692

Printed in Singapore by Sino Publishing on 150gsm Woodfree

9 8 7 6 5 4 3 2 1   99 00 01 02

Acknowledgments

This book would not have been written without the fantastic support
of Helen Littleton and the team at HarperCollins. Thanks.

My heartfelt thanks also to Jennifer Soo for the wonderful photography and great
doughnuts; to Yoshiko Takeuchi for tasting and assisting; to Annie Foord for giving
me the opportunity to manage the Sydney Seafood School (and for the
'honeyed ling' recipe!); to my good friend Jon Osbeiston for the wine suggestions;
to my family for understanding why I don't see them very often;
to my mentor Tetsuya Wakuda for not giving me any recipes and constantly telling
me to 'keep it simple'; and, of course, to Stefan – just for being you.

Introduction

After managing the Sydney Seafood School for two years,
I realised just how many people really wanted to learn how to cook seafood.
This is how **Seafood Kitchen** came about.

There are so many different ways of cooking seafood – and not cooking it!
My preference for cooking seafood is . . . keep it simple.
Fish and shellfish have delicate flavours and textures;
however you choose to prepare them, it's best to take it easy.

Each recipe in **Seafood Kitchen** is a meal, complete with serving suggestions
and condiments. I'd like my recipes to act as inspiration for you to be creative.
Taste regularly as you cook and add ingredients to suit your individual tastes.
I've made alternative suggestions for the recipes in case you can't find a
particular fish or shellfish; and the wine styles have been chosen by wine expert
Jon Osbeiston as a guide to enhancing the experience of your meal.

Enjoy!

Steaming & Poaching

Chinese-style Steamed Rock Cod

Poached Snapper with Sorrel Sauce

Flathead Fillets with Horseradish Cream

Poached Dory Fillets with Riesling Sauce

Whole Poached Atlantic Salmon with Dill Sauce

Steamed Prawns with Teriyaki Dipping Sauce

Crab & Soba Noodle Salad

Balmain Bugs with Rocket, Asparagus & Saffron Aïoli

Cold Squid Ink Pasta with Prawns, Capers & Lemon

Mussels Steamed in White Wine & Tarragon

Linguine with Clams

Marron & Potato Salad with Rich Dill Mayo

Coral Trout Fillets with Watercress & Pink Peppercorn Sauce

Steamed Scallops with Ginger & Coriander

Oysters Steamed with Ginger & Coriander

Pipis with Tomato, Saffron & Chilli Sauce

Steamed Mud Crabs with Champagne Sauce

Angelhair Pasta with Crab Sauce

Steaming

STEAMING cooks seafood with the heat of boiling liquid at a temperature higher than 100°C. It retains the flavour of the food and is ideal for delicate-flavoured seafood such as john dory and whiting. This cooking method is suitable for most firm-fleshed fish, including whole fish, fillets and cutlets.

Steaming is great for opening shellfish such as mussels and can be used for crustaceans such as lobsters, crabs, bugs and fresh-water crayfish.

Equipment

Bamboo steaming basket with a lid, placed over a wok or saucepan.

Stainless-steel fish kettle.

Stainless-steel saucepan with perforated steaming pan and lid.

Steaming oven.

Conventional oven using paper or aluminium foil parcel. The fish steams inside the parcel.

Improvise by placing seafood on a rack inside a baking dish with a small amount of liquid and cover tightly with aluminium foil.

How to steam

Bring liquid to the boil. Place the seafood in a single layer on the perforated surface of the steamer. Cover tightly and steam.

Check seafood at regular intervals to avoid overcooking.

If using a liquid marinade, place seafood on a plate that will fit easily inside the steamer. Allow sufficient room around the plate for the steam to rise and circulate.

Seafood can be steamed over plain water. You can add vegetables, herbs or citrus leaves to the liquid to give a subtle flavour to the steam.

POACHING requires covering the seafood with liquid and cooking below boiling point, between 70°C and 80°C. This is a gentle method of cooking that helps to retain the moisture of the flesh. It is suitable for almost any cut of firm-fleshed fish – it can be whole, in fillets or cutlets (for example, flathead, flounder and trevally).

Shellfish can be poached with or without the shells.

Equipment

Stainless-steel fish kettles are ideal for large, whole fish.

Alternatively, use any pan large enough to hold the seafood in a single layer, covered with liquid. A lid will help to prevent the liquid from evaporating.

How to poach

Place the seafood on a rack. This makes it easier to remove or place directly into the pan with poaching liquid.

Use just enough liquid to cover the seafood. This liquid can be salted water, herb-flavoured water, stock, court-bouillon, wine or milk.

Heat the poaching liquid to a gentle simmer (it should never reach the boil) and lower seafood into liquid. For large, whole fish, place into cooled liquid and slowly bring to a gentle simmer. Remove from the heat and allow the fish to sit in the cooling liquid. Check the fish occasionally. When the dorsal fin (the large fin in the centre of the back) comes away easily and the flesh flakes from the bone, the fish is done.

Poaching

Chinese-style Steamed Rock Cod

1 whole rock cod
(about 1.5 kg/3 lb), cleaned

4 tablespoons soy sauce

4 tablespoons Chinese rice wine

4 tablespoons sesame oil

1 teaspoon sugar

2 tablespoons finely grated ginger

4 spring onions, finely sliced

3 tablespoons finely chopped
coriander leaves

Bring a large saucepan of water to the boil and cover with a bamboo steamer.

Using a sharp knife, make 2 or 3 deep slits on both sides of the fish and place on a large, deep plate (the plate should fit inside the steamer basket). Combine the soy sauce, rice wine, sesame oil, sugar and ginger. Pour three-quarters of the liquid over the fish and top with spring onions and coriander leaves.

Place the plate inside the steamer basket, cover and steam for 15–20 minutes, or until the fish is cooked through.

Meanwhile, heat the remaining sauce in a small saucepan over medium heat.

To serve, place the fish on a large serving platter and pour over the remaining sauce. (For a little heat, add a small, finely chopped red chilli to the sauce.)

ALTERNATIVES
barramundi, silver bream, leatherjacket, snapper, rainbow trout, red emperor, red mullet

SERVES 4 AS A MAIN
PREPARATION TIME: 1 hour
WINE STYLE: oaked chardonnay

Poached Snapper
with Sorrel Sauce

1 large snapper
(about 1.5 kg / 3 lb), cleaned

COURT-BOUILLON
1 stalk celery, thinly sliced
1 large onion, sliced
4 sprigs parsley
1 small lemon, sliced
1 tablespoon black peppercorns

SORREL SAUCE
2 tablespoons unsalted butter
2 cloves garlic, finely chopped
2 spring onions, finely chopped
1/2 cup sorrel leaves
150 ml (1/2 cup) dry white wine
250 ml (1 cup) cream
salt and black pepper

Fill a fish-poaching kettle three-quarters full with water and add all the court-bouillon ingredients. Slowly bring to the boil, reduce the heat and simmer for 25 minutes. Remove the vegetables with a slotted spoon. Pour the liquid into a large bowl and set aside to cool.

Place the fish in the poaching kettle and cover with the cold court-bouillon. Cover with the lid and bring slowly to the boil. When the liquid starts to bubble, remove from the heat immediately. Leave the fish to cool in the court-bouillon without the lid. The fish will continue to cook and is ready when the dorsal fin pulls out easily.

For the sauce, melt the butter in a frying pan over medium heat. Add garlic and spring onions and sauté until softened. Add sorrel and sauté until softened. Add wine, raise the heat a little and cook until reduced by half. Stir in the cream and simmer until the sauce thickens slightly. Season to taste with salt and pepper.

Place the poached snapper on a large platter and pour over the sorrel sauce. Serve with steamed greens.

ALTERNATIVES
baby jewfish, coral trout, barramundi, rock cod, Murray cod, silver perch, snapper, red emperor, red mullet

Flathead Fillets with Horseradish Cream

**4 medium-sized flathead fillets
(about 200 g/7 oz each), skin removed**

125 ml (½ cup) water

2 tablespoons lemon juice

125 ml (½ cup) cream

2 large egg yolks, lightly beaten

**1 teaspoon
finely grated fresh horseradish
(see page 158)**

a pinch of white pepper

**1 bunch asparagus,
steamed and sliced**

In a frying pan over medium heat, place flathead fillets. Add water and lemon juice and gently poach for 5–6 minutes, or until the fillets are tender and cooked through. Transfer to a warm plate and keep warm.

Return the frying pan containing reserved liquid to the heat and reduce by half. Add the cream and egg yolks. Simmer for 2 minutes, stirring constantly, until thickened.

Add the horseradish and white pepper and simmer for a further minute.

To serve, place the fillets on serving plates and spoon over the sauce. Garnish with asparagus slices.

ALTERNATIVES
morwong, whiting, Atlantic salmon, warehou, mullet

6

Poached Dory Fillets with Riesling Sauce

2 tablespoons finely chopped shallots

150 ml (2/3 cup) riesling

125 ml (1/2 cup) fish stock (see page 158)

2 tablespoons chopped lemon thyme leaves

a pinch of sugar

4 medium-sized dory fillets (about 175 g/6 oz each), trimmed

200 g (7 oz) unsalted butter, cubed and chilled

salt and pepper

salmon roe for serving

Place the shallots, riesling, fish stock, lemon thyme and sugar in a large frying pan over medium heat. Cover and simmer for 5 minutes.

Add the dory fillets, cover and simmer gently for 8 minutes, or until just cooked. Remove the fillets, cover and keep warm until ready to serve.

Slowly bring the liquid to the boil and cook until reduced to a thick consistency. Strain through a fine-meshed sieve into a small saucepan and place over low heat. Whisk in the butter, a little at a time, until the sauce is smooth. Season with salt and pepper.

To serve, place the fillets on serving plates, spoon over a little of the sauce and top with a dollop of salmon roe.

ALTERNATIVES
snapper, morwong, sea perch, trout (all types), barramundi

Buying fish

Fish

Three basic rules apply when buying fish: look, smell and feel. With whole fish, look for bright, bulging eyes, glossy skin and tightly packed scales. The slime should be clear and the body firm. When pressed with your finger, the flesh should spring back. The fish should smell pleasantly of the sea.

For fillets, cutlets and steaks, look for bright, glossy flesh that is firmly attached to the bones (if there are any). The flesh should spring back when lightly prodded and it should be sweet smelling. Watch that the cut fish has not been sitting in water; the fish pieces should be relatively dry and not oozing water.

Shellfish

Again, let your nose, eyes and hands be your guide. With prawns, choose those with a pleasant smell, without any trace of ammonia. The heads and shells should be firm and glossy, and the flesh firm.

If possible, buy cooked prawns with their shells intact. Make sure there is no discolouration, particularly at the head and joints. The flesh should be firm and smell of the sea.

& shellfish

If you're buying crabs, pick them up from behind (easier if the claws are tied). With rock lobsters, bugs and freshwater crayfish such as yabbies and marron, pick them up firmly at the back of the head. With all shellfish, their legs should move when touched. The shells should be intact, with the heads and legs firmly attached to the body. The hard shells should be free of slime and grit, and they should be sweet smelling. Rock lobsters curl their tails under their body when picked up.

If you are buying chilled or cooked shellfish, look for intact shells with no discolouration or fading. The heads and legs must be firmly attached to the body, and the body free of slime and grit. The flesh should be very white, or a light cream colour, and smell of the ocean.

Scallops, whether bought on or off the shell, should have flesh that varies in colour from very white to cream. They should be plump and not dried out, with the orange fleshy roe firmly attached. The flesh should spring back when lightly pressed.

When buying live oysters and mussels, look for closed shells or those that close when tapped lightly. The shells should be intact and smell of the sea. Oyster meat is grey, male mussel flesh in usually white, and the female is bright orange.

If buying shucked oysters, the juices on the half shell should be lightly opalescent. Mussel juices should be clear. Both should be free of shell particles or sand. Look for plump, moist flesh that is springy to the touch.

Squid and octopus pigmentation vary according to the species. The skin should be intact and the flesh pure white in colour. They should have very firm flesh that is not slimy, and should smell of the ocean.

If possible, buy whole live abalone in their shells. The flesh should be firmly attached and the creamy white flesh firm to the touch. The dark pigment around the edge that is either black, brown or green in colour can be removed if desired. Abalone should smell pleasantly of the sea.

Whole Poached Atlantic Salmon with Dill Sauce

2 kg (4 lb) Atlantic salmon, cleaned

COURT-BOUILLON

150 ml ($\frac{2}{3}$ cup) dry white wine

3 fresh bay leaves

1 small onion, chopped

1 stalk celery, sliced

2 tablespoons chopped flat-leaf parsley

1 medium-sized carrot, sliced

4 sprigs fresh thyme, chopped

1 tablespoon whole black peppercorns

DILL SAUCE

375 ml ($1\frac{1}{2}$ cups) yoghurt

1 tablespoon olive oil

2 tablespoons finely chopped parsley

3 tablespoons finely chopped dill

1 tablespoon capers,
rinsed and finely chopped

2 cloves garlic, finely chopped

Fill a fish-poaching kettle three-quarters full with water and add all the court-bouillon ingredients. Slowly bring to the boil, reduce the heat and simmer for 25 minutes. Remove the vegetables with a slotted spoon. Pour the liquid into a large bowl and set aside to cool.

Place the fish in the poaching kettle and cover with the cold court-bouillon. Cover with the lid and bring slowly to the boil. When the liquid starts to bubble, remove from the heat immediately. Remove the lid and leave the fish to cool in the court-bouillon. The fish will continue to cook and is ready when the dorsal fin pulls out easily.

For the dill sauce, in a bowl combine the yoghurt, olive oil, parsley, dill, capers and garlic. Mix together thoroughly and set aside.

Remove the fish from the kettle and place on a large platter. With the back of a knife carefully remove the skin, leaving the head and tail intact. Gently turn the fish over and remove the rest of the skin.

Serve at room temperature with the sauce and some salad greens.

ALTERNATIVES
coral trout, snapper, emperor, barramundi, baby jewfish, ocean trout

Steamed Prawns with Teriyaki Dipping Sauce

SERVES 4 AS A STARTER
PREPARATION TIME: 15 minutes
WINE STYLE: medium-dry gewurztraminer

24 medium-sized green (raw) tiger prawns, shelled and deveined

DIPPING SAUCE
60 ml (¼ cup) mirin (see page 159)
60 ml (¼ cup) soy sauce
60 ml (¼ cup) sake (see page 159)
1 tablespoon sugar
½ teaspoon peeled and grated ginger
½ teaspoon minced garlic

For the dipping sauce, combine mirin, soy sauce, sake and sugar in a small saucepan. Slowly bring to the boil, stirring constantly for about 3 minutes. Remove from the heat and add ginger and garlic. Set aside to cool.

Place a bamboo steamer over a half-filled saucepan of boiling water. Arrange peeled prawns on a plate smaller than the inside of the steamer. Cover and steam for 3–4 minutes or until the prawns turn pink. Remove prawns from the steamer and serve immediately with the dipping sauce.

ALTERNATIVES
bugs, calamari, cuttlefish, scallops, mussels, abalone

11

Crab & Soba Noodle Salad

2 large green (raw) blue swimmer crabs (about 450 g/14 oz each)

250 g (8 oz) dried soba noodles (see page 160)

2 tablespoons black sesame seeds (see page 156)

2 medium-sized spring onions, chopped

DRESSING

80 ml (1/3 cup) grapeseed oil

1 tablespoon lime juice

1 tablespoon soy sauce

1/2 teaspoon sugar

Bring a large saucepan of water to a gentle simmer. Add the crabs and cook for 5–6 minutes (10 minutes if using mud crabs), or until the shells turn bright orange in colour.

Cut the cooked crab into quarters and pick the meat from the body and legs. Discard all shells. Cover and refrigerate until ready to use.

Place the noodles in a saucepan of boiling water. When the water returns to the boil, add an additional cup of cold water and continue to boil for 8 minutes, or until al dente. Drain and set aside to cool.

Combine the crab meat with black sesame seeds and set aside.

For the dressing, combine the grapeseed oil, lime juice, soy sauce and sugar. Mix together well.

Toss the noodles in the dressing. Place noodles on serving plates, top with crab meat and sprinkle with spring onions.

ALTERNATIVES
bugs, freshwater crayfish (eg yabbies, marron), prawns, scallops, calamari

Balmain Bugs with Rocket, Asparagus & Saffron Aïoli

SERVES 4 AS A STARTER

PREPARATION TIME: 25 minutes

WINE STYLE: full-bodied sauvignon blanc

8 large green (raw) Balmain bugs (about 150 g/5 oz each)

2 bunches rocket, trimmed

1 bunch asparagus, steamed and sliced

AÏOLI

2 cloves garlic, finely chopped

3 large egg yolks

1 tablespoon lemon juice

salt and pepper

175 ml (³/4 cup) olive oil

a pinch of saffron threads, soaked in 1 tablespoon water

Place the bugs in a saucepan of cold water. Slowly bring to a gentle simmer and cook until they turn bright orange, about 4 minutes.

Remove the bugs from the water and set aside to cool. Slice each bug lengthways and remove the meat from the shells.

For the aïoli, place the garlic, egg yolks, lemon juice, salt and pepper in a food processor or blender and blend well. With the motor running, gradually pour in the olive oil and blend until thickened. Pour into a small bowl and stir in the saffron and its soaking liquid.

Arrange rocket leaves and asparagus on serving plates and top with the bugs. Drizzle over the aïoli and serve.

ALTERNATIVES
prawns, scallops, freshwater crayfish (eg yabbies, marron), mussels, oysters, calamari

Cold Squid Ink Pasta with Prawns, Capers & Lemon

SERVES 4 AS A STARTER
PREPARATION TIME: 20 minutes
WINE STYLE: dry riesling

250 g (8 oz) squid ink pasta

1 kg (2 lb) medium-sized green (raw) prawns

2 tablespoons capers, finely chopped

1 tablespoon finely chopped parsley

3 tablespoons olive oil

1 tablespoon lemon juice

2 teaspoons lemon zest

cracked black pepper

Place the pasta in a saucepan of boiling water and cook until al dente. Strain and set aside.

Place a steamer basket over a saucepan of boiling water. Arrange prawns on a plate smaller than the inside of the steamer basket. Place the plate of prawns inside steamer, cover and cook until prawns have turned pink. Remove the shells, devein and set aside.

In a bowl, toss together the capers, parsley, oil and lemon juice.

Arrange pasta on serving plates and top with prawns and oil mixture. Garnish with lemon zest and cracked black pepper.

ALTERNATIVES
scallops, bugs, calamari, cuttlefish,
freshwater crayfish (eg yabbies, marron)

SERVES 4 AS MAIN

PREPARATION TIME: 15 minutes

WINE STYLE: dry chenin blanc

Mussels Steamed in White Wine & Tarragon

1 kg (2 lb) mussels, scrubbed

1 tablespoon olive oil

3 small spring onions, finely chopped

3 cloves garlic, finely chopped

250 ml (1 cup) dry white wine

125 ml (½ cup) fish stock (see page 158)

4 tablespoons chopped tarragon

Remove beards from the mussels and discard any that have opened or have broken shells. Set aside.

Heat olive oil over medium heat in a large frying pan or wok. Add spring onions and garlic and cook until softened. Add wine, stock, tarragon and mussels. Cover and cook for 2–3 minutes, or until the shells have opened. Remove the mussels from the liquid with a pair of tongs and place in a large bowl. Discard any that have not opened.

Strain the liquid through a fine-meshed sieve and pour over the mussels. Serve immediately with crusty bread.

ALTERNATIVES

clams, pipis, green prawns, green bugs, scallops

Linguine with Clams

1.5 kg (3 lb) clams, scrubbed
250 g (8 oz) linguine
3 tablespoons olive oil
3 cloves garlic, finely chopped
150 ml (⅔ cup) dry white wine
½ cup chopped parsley
sea salt and black pepper

Place the scrubbed clams in a bowl of water and soak for an hour or so to remove sand and grit.

Bring a saucepan of water to the boil and cook the linguine until al dente. Drain and set aside.

Heat the olive oil in a large frying pan over medium heat. Add the garlic and cook until fragrant. Add wine, clams, parsley, salt and pepper. Cover and simmer for 2–3 minutes, or until clams have opened. Discard any that have not opened.

Place the linguine in the frying pan and toss with the sauce. Serve immediately with cracked black pepper.

ALTERNATIVES
· mussels, clams, green (raw) prawns, cuttlefish, calamari, scallops

SERVES 4 AS A STARTER

PREPARATION TIME: 25 minutes

WINE STYLE: medium-bodied chardonnay

Marron & Potato Salad with Rich Dill Mayo

500 g (1 lb) potatoes, peeled

4 medium-sized marron (about 250 g/8 oz each)

2 large egg yolks

1 large egg

2 teaspoons Dijon mustard

1 tablespoon lemon juice

a pinch of salt

2 pinches white pepper

375 ml (1½ cups) vegetable oil or olive oil

3 tablespoons chopped dill

Boil the potatoes until tender. Drain and set aside to cool.

Place marron in a saucepan of cold water. Slowly bring to a simmer and cook until the shells turn bright orange, about 5–6 minutes. Remove from the water and set aside to cool. Slice each marron lengthways and remove the meat from the shells. Cut into large chunks and set aside.

In a food processor, combine the egg yolks, egg, mustard, lemon juice, salt and pepper. Process for 1 minute. With the motor running, gradually pour in the oil and continue to process until thickened. Taste and adjust the seasoning, if necessary. Pour the mayonnaise into a container, stir in 2 tablespoons of dill and refrigerate until ready to use.

When the potatoes are cool, cut into a large dice. Pour over enough mayonnaise to coat the potatoes lightly. Add the marron and gently toss together. To serve, place salad in a large bowl and sprinkle with the remaining dill.

ALTERNATIVES
yabbies, prawns, bugs, calamari, abalone

Coral Trout Fillets with Watercress & Pink Peppercorn Sauce

SERVES 4 AS A MAIN

PREPARATION TIME: 30 minutes

WINE STYLE: lightly oaked marsanne

PINK PEPPERCORN SAUCE

1 tablespoon tomato paste

1 teaspoon Dijon mustard

2 tablespoons lemon juice

2 tablespoons pink peppercorns in brine, drained (see page 159)

1 tablespoon butter

1 medium-sized onion, finely chopped

1 cup cream

salt and pepper

4 coral trout fillets (about 200 g/7 oz each), trimmed

1 bunch watercress, trimmed

For the sauce, place the tomato paste, mustard, lemon juice and pink peppercorns in a food processor and blend together until a smooth paste forms. Set aside.

In a frying pan, melt butter over medium heat. Add onion and cook until softened. Add pink peppercorn mixture and combine well. Add cream and simmer for 3–4 minutes, or until the sauce reduces slightly. Season to taste with salt and pepper.

Meanwhile, line a bamboo steamer basket with aluminium foil and lightly brush with oil or butter. Arrange the fillets inside the steamer. Cover and steam for 10–12 minutes or until the fillets are cooked through and soft to the touch.

To serve, place the steamed fillets onto warm serving plates. Spoon over a small amount of sauce and pile with watercress.

ALTERNATIVES
Atlantic salmon, ocean trout, blue eye, boneless fillets, barramundi, ling, gemfish

21

SERVES 4 AS A STARTER
PREPARATION TIME: 10 minutes
WINE STYLE: unoaked semillon

Steamed Scallops
with Ginger & Coriander

4 tablespoons grapeseed oil

1 teaspoon finely chopped ginger

2 tablespoons soy sauce

1 tablespoon finely chopped coriander

12 large scallops on the half shell

Bring a large saucepan of water to the boil. Cover with a bamboo steaming basket.

In a bowl, combine the grapeseed oil, ginger, soy sauce and coriander. Spoon the sauce over the scallops.

Arrange the scallops inside the steaming basket (you may have to steam them in batches). Steam for 3–4 minutes or until just cooked. Serve immediately on warm serving plates.

ALTERNATIVES
prawns, cuttlefish, calamari (squid), abalone, oysters

SERVES 4 AS A STARTER
PREPARATION TIME: 10 minutes
WINE STYLE: dry unwooded chardonnay

Oysters Steamed
with Ginger & Coriander

1 teaspoon finely chopped ginger

4 tablespoons grapeseed oil

2 tablespoons light soy sauce

**3 medium-sized spring onions,
green stems only, finely sliced**

16 large Pacific oysters on the half shell

**2 tablespoons finely chopped
coriander leaves**

In a bowl, combine the ginger, grapeseed oil, soy sauce and spring onions. Spoon sauce over freshly shucked oysters.

Place the steamer basket over a saucepan of boiling water. Carefully arrange oysters in the basket and steam for 1–2 minutes, or until just warmed through.

Remove oysters from the steamer, sprinkle with coriander and serve immediately.

ALTERNATIVES
scallops, pipis, clams, mussels, prawns, calamari

SERVES 4 AS A STARTER

PREPARATION TIME: 40 minutes

WINE STYLE: sauvignon blanc

Pipis with Tomato, Saffron & Chilli Sauce

1.5 kg (3 lb) pipis, scrubbed

3 tablespoons olive oil

1 small onion, finely chopped

2 cloves garlic, finely chopped

1 stalk celery, chopped

6 medium-sized tomatoes, chopped

1 tablespoon tomato paste

80 ml (1/3 cup) dry white wine

1 small red chilli, seeded and chopped

a pinch of saffron threads

150 ml (2/3 cup) water

2 tablespoons chopped parsley

Place the pipis in a bowl of water and soak for an hour or so to remove sand and grit.

Heat the olive oil in a large frying pan over medium heat. Add the onion, garlic and celery and cook until softened. Add the tomatoes, tomato paste, white wine, chilli, saffron and water. Simmer for 10–15 minutes or until thickened. Add the parsley, stirring thoroughly.

Drain pipis and add to the sauce. Cook for about 10 minutes or until pipis have opened. Discard any that have not opened. Serve immediately with crusty bread.

ALTERNATIVES
mussels, clams, baby octopus, calamari, cuttlefish

Steamed Mud Crabs with Champagne Sauce

2 large live mud crabs

2 tablespoons butter

1 small golden shallot, chopped

1 tablespoon chopped thyme leaves

250 ml (1 cup) champagne

125 ml (½ cup) fish stock (see page 158)

60 ml (¼ cup) cream

2 egg yolks

salt and cracked black pepper

To kill the crabs, place in a freezer for 1 hour or until the crabs are 'asleep'. Cut the crabs into quarters and crack claws with a nut cracker or the back of a heavy knife.

Melt the butter in a large saucepan over medium heat. Add the shallots and cook until softened. Add the crab and thyme and cook for 4–5 minutes or until the shells just change colour.

Add the champagne and stock, cover and simmer for another 5 minutes. Remove from the heat and set aside.

Remove crabs from sauce and set aside. Add cream and egg yolks to the sauce and whisk together well. Return the sauce to a low heat, season with salt and black pepper and cook for a further 2 minutes.

To serve, place crab pieces on serving plates, pour the champagne sauce over the top and sprinkle with freshly ground black pepper.

ALTERNATIVES
blue swimmer crabs, live or uncooked spanner crabs, bugs, yabbies, prawns

Angelhair Pasta with Crab Sauce

4 medium-sized green (raw) blue swimmer crabs (about 400 g/14 oz each)

400 g (14 oz) angelhair pasta (see page 156)

4 tablespoons olive oil

2 cloves garlic, finely chopped

4 large ripe tomatoes, diced

2 tablespoons finely chopped basil

1 tablespoon finely chopped oregano

250 ml (1 cup) cream

salt and pepper

Bring a large saucepan of water to the boil and cover with a bamboo steaming basket. Place the whole crabs inside the basket, cover and steam for 8–10 minutes, or until the shells have turned a bright orange. Remove from the heat and when cool, cut into segments and remove the flesh. Discard shells.

Meanwhile, place the pasta in a saucepan of boiling water and cook until al dente. Drain well and set aside.

Heat olive oil in a frying pan over medium heat. Add the garlic and cook for 2 minutes. Add tomatoes, basil and oregano and simmer for 10 minutes or until reduced to a thick pulpy sauce.

When tomato sauce is ready pour in the cream, season with salt and pepper and combine thoroughly. Add crab meat and simmer for a further 2–3 minutes.

Remove the crab sauce from the heat and pour into a saucepan with pasta. Mix together thoroughly with a wooden spoon. Serve immediately.

ALTERNATIVES
prawns, bugs, scallops, calamari, cuttlefish, mussels

Deep-frying, Stir-frying, & Pan-frying

Crispy Flathead with Sweet Potato Chips
& Rocket Salad

Blue Eye with Caramelised Peppers

Deep-fried Garfish with Bacon & Basil

Fried Whitebait with Pear & Rocket Salad

Chilli Crab

Flounder Fillets with Warm Bean Salad

Garfish filled with Sage & Onion

Pan-fried Skate with Harissa Butter

Garfish with Steamed Asparagus
& Sage Butter

Red Emperor with Buttered Spinach
& Red Wine Sauce

Pan-fried Trout with Olives & Capers

Abalone with Garlic Butter

Garlic & Chilli Prawns

Mussels with Tomato & Basil

Mud Crab with Roasted Tomato
& Tarragon Sauce

Cuttlefish with Noodles & Black Bean Sauce

Sautéed Squid with Soy & Butter

Salt & Pepper Crab

Pasta with Prawns & Prosciutto

Prawns in a Coconut Curry Sauce

Seared Scallops with Daikon Salad

Stir-fried Squid with Shiitake & Bok Choy

Stir-fried Abalone with Chinese Greens

Thai Cuttlefish Salad

Yabbies Fried in Orange & Basil

Warm Salad of Bay Prawns & Broad Beans

King Prawn Rice Paper Rolls

Dory Fillets with Apple & Cucumber Salsa

Frying

DEEP-FRYING, STIR-FRYING AND SHALLOW-FRYING seafood in oils or butter is relatively fast, and the heat you are cooking with is easily controlled.

Frying by any of these methods suits almost all whole fish, fillets and cutlets. Deep-frying, stir-frying and shallow-frying are also ideal for octopus, squid and shellfish such as prawns.

Equipment

A thermostatically controlled deep-fryer or wok.

Any flat, heavy-based pan for pan-frying.

A wok or large-based pan for stir-frying.

How to fry

Deep-frying seafood in clean, hot oil between 170°C and 180°C is best when seafood has a coating such as flour, breadcrumbs or batter. The coating seals in the moisture and stops the oil entering the seafood. To test the heat of the oil, place a small amount of batter in hot oil. It should sizzle and turn golden within 30 seconds.

When deep-frying, cook only a small amount at a time. Lower the seafood into oil with tongs or in a frying basket. When cooked, drain excess oil on absorbent paper. Before cooking the next batch, allow the oil to return to its controlled temperature.

To pan-fry, heat oil or butter (or a mixture of both) in the pan. Place the fish, presentation-side down, and cook over medium to high heat. The cooking time will vary depending on the thickness of the fish and whether you prefer the fish to be cooked through. Turn fish only once; very thin fillets can be cooked on one side only.

Stir-frying requires seafood to be cut into thin, equal-sized pieces for fast and even cooking. Add the ingredients in the order of the longest cooking time first, to ensure that all ingredients are cooked for the right length of time.

Crispy Flathead with Sweet Potato Chips & Rocket Salad

SERVES 4 AS A MAIN

PREPARATION TIME: 45 minutes

WINE STYLE: dry unoaked semillon

400 g (14 oz) sweet potato, peeled

olive oil

155 g (1 cup) self-raising flour

125 ml (½ cup) beer

250 ml (1 cup) cold water

a pinch of white pepper

oil for deep-frying

4 flathead fillets, skinned, boned and halved crosswise

1 bunch rocket, trimmed

2 tablespoons olive oil

1 tablespoon balsamic vinegar

cracked black pepper

Preheat oven to 200°C.

Slice the sweet potato into 5 mm (⅛ in) rounds and arrange in a shallow baking tray. Drizzle with olive oil and bake for 30 minutes or until crispy. Cover and set aside.

For the batter, whisk together the flour, beer, water and pepper until smooth.

Heat oil over high heat in a deep frying pan. To test if the oil is ready, drop a small amount of the batter into the oil. The batter should sizzle and turn golden immediately. If the batter burns, reduce the heat and test again.

Coat each fillet lightly in the batter and drop into hot oil. Cook each fillet for 2 minutes or until golden. Drain on paper towels.

Combine the rocket, olive oil and vinegar.

To serve, place the crispy flathead and sweet potato chips on serving plates and place a rocket salad to the side. Season with cracked black pepper.

ALTERNATIVES
boneless fillets, ling, blue grenadier, whiting, ocean perch, sea perch, gemfish

31

Blue Eye with Caramelised Peppers

3 tablespoons olive oil

1 large green capsicum, seeded and sliced

1 large red capsicum, seeded and sliced

1 large yellow capsicum, seeded and sliced

1 tablespoon sugar

2 tablespoons capers, drained and chopped

3 tablespoons chopped basil leaves

4 blue eye fillets (about 200 g/7 oz each), trimmed

cracked black pepper

baby English spinach leaves for serving

Heat oil over medium heat in a frying pan. Add the green, red and yellow capsicums and sauté for 3–4 minutes or until softened.

Add sugar, capers and basil and cook for a further 2 minutes. Remove from the heat. Remove the capsicum mixture with a pair of tongs and set aside. Reserve the pan juices.

Place the fillets into the frying pan with the reserved juices. Season with black pepper and cook over medium heat for 3–4 minutes on each side or until the fish is just cooked through.

Arrange the spinach leaves on serving plates and top with the fish. Serve with a small pile of caramelised peppers.

ALTERNATIVES
ling, boneless fillets, barramundi, Atlantic salmon, ocean trout, jewfish

Deep-fried Garfish with Bacon & Basil

16 medium-sized garfish fillets, trimmed

8 thin rashers bacon, halved crossways

16 large basil leaves

310 g (2 cups) plain flour

500 ml (2 cups) iced water

2 large egg yolks

grapeseed oil for deep-frying

sea salt and cracked black pepper

Place the garfish on a flat dry surface and top with bacon and basil. Roll garfish towards the tail and secure with a toothpick. Repeat with the remaining garfish.

In a large bowl, combine the flour, water and egg yolks. Mix together gently with a fork and set aside.

Heat oil in a deep pan over high heat.

Dip the rolled garfish in batter and deep-fry, two at a time, until golden. Drain on paper towels.

Serve seasoned with sea salt and cracked pepper.

ALTERNATIVES
whiting, dory, flounder, trevally

SERVES 4 AS A STARTER
PREPARATION TIME: 30 minutes
WINE STYLE: cool-climate sauvignon blanc

Fried Whitebait with Pear & Rocket Salad

grapeseed oil for frying

750 g (1½ lb) whitebait, washed and dried

plain flour for coating

1 medium-sized ripe pear, thinly sliced

1 bunch rocket, stems removed

1 tablespoon lemon juice

2 tablespoons grapeseed oil

1 teaspoon sansho pepper (see page 159)

1 tablespoon sea salt

Heat the oil in a frying pan over high heat. Lightly coat the whitebait in flour and add to the hot oil. It's best to cook in batches so the temperature of the oil doesn't drop too quickly.

Remove with a slotted spoon and drain on paper towels.

In a bowl combine the pear, rocket, lemon juice and grapeseed oil.

Divide the fried whitebait between 4 serving plates and place the salad to one side. Combine the sansho pepper and sea salt and sprinkle over the fish.

ALTERNATIVES
whiting, sardines (pilchards), flathead fillets, ocean perch fillets, garfish

Chilli Crab

**3 medium-sized green (raw)
blue swimmer crabs
(about 400 g/14 oz each), cleaned**

2 tablespoons olive oil

1 tablespoon sesame oil

3 cloves garlic, finely chopped

**1 tablespoon peeled
and chopped ginger**

2 small red chillies, chopped

3 tablespoons sweet chilli sauce

2 tablespoons light soy sauce

1 tablespoon hoisin sauce

1 teaspoon sugar

Chop each crab into 4 segments (6 if the crabs are large). Crack the claws with a nut cracker or the back of a heavy knife.

Heat the olive oil and the sesame oil in a wok over high heat. Add the garlic, ginger and chilli and cook for 1–2 minutes until fragrant. Add the chilli sauce, soy sauce, hoisin sauce and sugar. Cook for a further 4–5 minutes.

Add the crab and coat thoroughly in sauce. Stir-fry for a further 5–7 minutes or until the shells turn bright orange and the crabs are cooked through. Serve on a large platter.

ALTERNATIVES
mud crab, prawns, calamari (squid), octopus, abalone, bugs

SERVES 4 AS A MAIN
PREPARATION TIME: 30 minutes
WINE STYLE: medium-bodied chardonnay

Flounder Fillets with Warm Bean Salad

2 tablespoons butter
150 g (5 oz) green beans, trimmed
150 g (5 oz) snake beans, cut in half
4 slices pancetta
2 tablespoons chopped parsley
4 flounder fillets (about 200 g / 7 oz each)
freshly ground black pepper

Melt half the butter in a frying pan over medium heat. Add the beans, pancetta and parsley and cook for 2–3 minutes or until tender. Remove the frying pan from the heat and, with a slotted spoon, transfer the beans and pancetta to a warm dish.

Return the frying pan to the heat and melt the remaining butter. Place the fillets in the pan and cook for 1–2 minutes on each side or until just cooked.

Place the fillets on warm plates and serve with warm bean salad and freshly ground pepper.

ALTERNATIVES
dory, snapper, morwong, sea perch, Atlantic salmon, trout

Garfish filled with Sage & Onion

2 tablespoons butter

1 large onion, finely chopped

2 cloves garlic, finely chopped

1 cup fresh breadcrumbs

4 large sage leaves, finely chopped

2 tablespoons finely chopped parsley

1 large egg, beaten

12 medium-sized garfish, gutted and backbone removed*

plain flour for coating

grapeseed oil for frying

lemon wedges

* ask your fishmonger to do this for you

Melt butter in a frying pan over medium heat. Add onion and garlic and sauté until softened. Remove from the heat and transfer to a bowl. Add the breadcrumbs, sage, parsley and egg and combine thoroughly.

Spoon the filling into the cavity of each garfish and secure with toothpicks.

Lightly coat each garfish in flour and shallow-fry in hot grapeseed oil for 1–2 minutes on each side.

To serve, remove the toothpicks and place on serving plates with lemon wedges.

ALTERNATIVES
whiting, rainbow trout, silver bream, snapper, Murray cod, silver perch, baby barramundi

SERVES 4 AS A MAIN

PREPARATION TIME: 20 minutes

WINE STYLE: medium-dry riesling

Pan-fried Skate with Harissa Butter

HARISSA BUTTER

100 g (3½ oz) butter, diced

2 large fresh red chillies, seeded and chopped

1 small red capsicum, seeded and chopped

juice of 1 small lemon

2 cloves garlic, chopped

1 teaspoon salt

1 teaspoon ground cumin

1 teaspoon caraway seeds

4 large mint leaves

⅓ cup coriander leaves

4 skate fillets (about 180 g/6 oz each), skinned and trimmed

salt and pepper

butter for frying

baby spinach leaves for serving

lemon wedges for serving

To make the harissa butter, place butter, chillies, capsicum, lemon juice, garlic, salt, cumin, caraway seeds, mint and coriander in a food processor and process into a smooth thick paste. Add a little extra butter if the mixture is too dry.

Place a sheet of foil or greaseproof paper on a flat surface and spoon the butter into the centre to form a cylinder about 4 cm (1½ in) in width. Wrap tightly and place in the refrigerator or freezer until firm. Harissa butter can be stored in the refrigerator for up to one week or frozen for one month.

Season the skate with salt and pepper and set aside.

Heat butter in a frying pan over medium heat, add the skate fillets and cook for 2 minutes on each side or until the flesh just turns opaque.

Remove the butter from the refrigerator and slice into 5 mm (⅛ in) discs.

Place the fish on serving plates and top with the butter. Serve with baby spinach and lemon wedges.

ALTERNATIVES
boneless fillets, ling, blue eye, tuna, swordfish, gemfish

Garfish with Steamed Asparagus & Sage Butter

SERVES 4 AS A MAIN

PREPARATION TIME: 35 minutes

WINE STYLE: full-bodied chardonnay

2 bunches asparagus, trimmed

100 g (3½ oz) unsalted butter

1 clove garlic, finely chopped

12 fresh sage leaves

12 medium-sized garfish, cleaned

cracked black pepper

Bring a saucepan of water to the boil and cover with a bamboo steamer. Place the asparagus in the steamer and steam until tender. Cover and set aside in a warm place.

Meanwhile, melt the butter over medium heat in a frying pan. Add the garlic and sage leaves and allow the butter to bubble gently.

Place the garfish into the frying pan and cook for 1–2 minutes on each side or until just cooked. Remove each garfish from the frying pan. Reserve the butter.

To serve, place the asparagus on serving plates and top with the garfish. Pour over the butter and sprinkle with cracked black pepper.

ALTERNATIVES
whiting, blue mackerel, sardines (pilchards), rainbow trout

40

Red Emperor with Buttered Spinach & Red Wine Sauce

SERVES 4 AS A MAIN

PREPARATION TIME: 35 minutes

WINE STYLE: soft, light-bodied shiraz

3 tablespoons butter

1 small onion, finely chopped

1 stalk celery, finely chopped

2 tablespoons finely chopped thyme leaves

500 ml (2 cups) red wine

375 ml (1½ cups) fish stock (see page 158)

1 tablespoon plain flour

1 tablespoon butter, extra

1 bunch English spinach, trimmed and blanched

salt and pepper

4 red emperor fillets (about 175 g/6 oz each), trimmed

Melt 2 tablespoons of butter in a large saucepan over medium heat. Add the onion, celery and thyme and sauté until softened. Pour in the wine and stock and slowly bring to the boil. Simmer gently until the liquid has reduced by half, about 5 minutes.

Blend together the remaining butter and flour and whisk into the liquid, a little at a time. Remove from the heat and keep warm.

Melt the butter in another frying pan over medium heat. Add the blanched spinach and season with salt and pepper. Toss the spinach gently in the butter and remove with a slotted spoon. Set aside in a warm place.

Place the red emperor fillets in the frying pan with the remaining butter and pan-fry for 2 minutes on each side, or until the fish turns opaque and is just cooked.

Divide the spinach between serving plates and top with the fish. Spoon a little red wine sauce around the fish and serve immediately.

ALTERNATIVES
snapper, Atlantic salmon, ocean trout, blue eye, ling, barramundi, gemfish

41

Pan-fried Trout
with Olives & Capers

SERVES 4 AS A MAIN
PREPARATION TIME: 30 minutes
WINE STYLE: lightly oaked marsanne

plain flour for coating

salt and pepper

**4 small whole trout
(about 300 g/10 oz each), cleaned**

125 g (4 oz) butter

2 cloves garlic, finely chopped

**2 tablespoons capers,
rinsed and chopped**

**1 cup black olives, stones removed,
finely chopped**

2 tablespoons chopped oregano

Sprinkle the flour on a large plate and season with salt and pepper. Lightly coat each trout with the flour.

Melt half the butter in a frying pan over medium heat. Place two trout in the melted butter and cook for 2–3 minutes on each side or until cooked through. Remove from the pan, place on a plate and cover with aluminium foil to keep warm.

Add the remaining butter to the pan and repeat for the remaining trout. Keep warm.

Add garlic to the pan and sauté until golden. Add the capers, black olives and oregano and sauté for a further 2 minutes.

Place the fish on warmed serving plates and spoon over the olive and caper mixture. Serve with roasted potatoes and lemon wedges.

ALTERNATIVES
baby barramundi, leatherjackets, small snapper, garfish, whiting

42

SERVES 4 AS A STARTER
PREPARATION TIME: 20 minutes
WINE STYLE: medium-bodied chardonnay

Abalone with Garlic Butter

2 large abalone steaks, thinly sliced diagonally

salt and white pepper

4 tablespoons butter

2 cloves garlic, finely chopped

2 tablespoons white wine

1 tablespoon finely chopped parsley

Season the abalone slices with salt and pepper.

Melt the butter in a frying pan over medium heat. Place the abalone in the frying pan and sauté for 30 seconds on each side. Remove the abalone when done and place on warm plates.

Add the garlic to the hot pan and cook for 1 minute. Add the white wine and parsley and bring to a quick simmer. Spoon the sauce over the abalone slices and serve immediately.

ALTERNATIVES
scallops, calamari (squid), bugs, prawns

PREPARATION TIME: 20 minutes
WINE STYLE: medium-dry riesling

Garlic & Chilli Prawns

250 ml (1 cup) olive oil

125 ml (½ cup) white wine

4 cloves garlic, finely chopped

1 small red chilli, finely chopped

1 teaspoon cracked black pepper

1.5 kg (3 lb) green (raw) endeavour prawns, shelled and deveined, tails intact

2 tablespoons finely chopped parsley

Heat the oil and white wine over high heat in a frying pan. Add the garlic, chilli and black pepper and cook for 1–2 minutes. When the oil is very hot, add the prawns and cook until just pink. Remove the prawns from the oil with a pair of tongs and place in warm serving bowls.

Pour over the oil mixture and sprinkle with parsley. Serve with crusty bread.

ALTERNATIVES
crabs, bugs, freshwater crayfish, mussels, calamari (squid), baby octopus

Mussels with Tomato & Basil

1.5 kg (3 lb) mussels, scrubbed

2 tablespoons olive oil

1 large onion, chopped

3 cloves garlic, chopped

2 x 440 g (14½ oz) tins of tomatoes, chopped

1 tablespoon tomato paste

1 tablespoon finely chopped parsley

4 tablespoons finely chopped basil

1 teaspoon sugar

salt and pepper

Remove the beards from the mussels.

Heat the olive oil in a frying pan and sauté the onion and garlic until tender. Add the tomatoes, tomato paste, parsley, basil, sugar, salt and pepper and slowly bring to the boil. Simmer for 5–10 minutes or until thickened. Add the mussels, cover and cook until the shells open. Discard any that do not open.

Ladle the mussels and sauce into deep serving bowls and serve immediately.

ALTERNATIVES
prawns, clams, pipis, baby octopus

Mud Crab with Roasted Tomato & Tarragon Sauce

SERVES 4 AS A MAIN
PREPARATION TIME: 1 hour 10 minutes
WINE STYLE: dry rosé

2 large live green mud crabs
(about 1 kg/2 lb each)
250 g (8 oz) roma tomatoes, halved
2 cloves garlic, thinly sliced
a pinch of sugar
1/3 cup chopped tarragon leaves
4 tablespoons olive oil
salt and pepper

Place the crabs in a freezer for 1 hour or until they are 'asleep'.

Preheat the oven to 180°C.

Arrange the tomatoes and garlic in a roasting pan. Sprinkle over the sugar and half the tarragon leaves. Drizzle with olive oil and roast for 40 minutes, or until the tomatoes are very soft. Remove from the oven and set aside to cool.

Place the roasted tomatoes and remaining tarragon in a food processor and process until smooth. Push the sauce through a fine-meshed sieve into a saucepan, add 125 ml (½ cup) of water and cook over medium heat for 5 minutes. Season with salt and pepper to taste.

Remove the crabs from the freezer and cut into quarters. Gently rinse under cold water.

Add crabs to the sauce and simmer for 10–15 minutes, or until the shells have changed colour and the flesh is just cooked through.

To serve, place the crab in serving bowls, pour over the sauce and serve immediately.

ALTERNATIVES
blue swimmer crabs, mussels, baby octopus, prawns

Cuttlefish with Noodles & Black Bean Sauce

8 medium-sized cuttlefish, cleaned

1 tablespoon black beans, salted, rinsed and chopped

1 clove garlic, finely chopped

2 teaspoons finely grated ginger

1 tablespoon light soy sauce

500 g (1 lb) Hokkien noodles (see page 158)

4 tablespoons peanut oil

2 medium-sized spring onions, chopped

Slice the cuttlefish into thin strips. Cover and refrigerate until ready to use. Combine the black beans, garlic, ginger and soy sauce in a mixing bowl.

Meanwhile, cover the noodles with boiling water and let stand for 3–4 minutes. Drain well.

Heat the oil in a wok over high heat. Add the black bean mixture and cook for 1 minute. Add the cuttlefish, coat well with the sauce and stir-fry for 1 minute. Add the noodles and stir-fry for a further 2 minutes. To serve, place noodles on serving plates and sprinkle with spring onions.

ALTERNATIVES
baby octopus, prawns, calamari (squid)

Salt & Pepper Crab

125 ml (½ cup) peanut oil

4 cloves garlic, finely chopped

2 teaspoons finely chopped ginger

4 medium-sized green
(raw) blue swimmer crabs
(about 400 g/14 oz each), segmented

3 teaspoons ground rock salt

3 teaspoons ground white peppercorns

6 small spring onions, chopped

2 teaspoons sugar

2½ tablespoons Chinese rice wine

Heat peanut oil in a wok over high heat. Add the garlic, ginger, crabs, salt and pepper and cook for 4–5 minutes.

Meanwhile, combine the spring onions, sugar and rice wine and pour over the crab. Coat thoroughly with the mixture. Cook for a further 2–3 minutes or until the shells turn bright orange and the flesh is tender. Arrange the crabs on a large platter and serve immediately.

ALTERNATIVES
prawns, bugs, freshwater crayfish (eg yabbies and marron), scampi, cuttlefish

Sautéed Squid with Soy & Butter

4 tablespoons butter

1 tablespoon soy sauce

500 g (1 lb) squid, cut into strips

2 tablespoons chopped chives

Heat the butter in a frying pan or wok over medium heat. Add the soy sauce and combine well.

Add the squid and sauté until just cooked, about 3 minutes.

To serve, divide the squid between 4 serving plates, spoon over the butter and sprinkle with chives.

ALTERNATIVES
cuttlefish, baby octopus, crabs, bugs, royal red prawns

Pasta with Prawns & Prosciutto

500 g (1 lb) fettuccine

3 tablespoons olive oil

2 cloves garlic, finely chopped

6 slices prosciutto

1 tablespoon chopped fresh oregano

750 g (1½ lb) green (raw) banana prawns, peeled and deveined

cracked black pepper

Place fettuccine in a saucepan of boiling water and cook until al dente. Drain and set aside.

Heat olive oil in a large frying pan or wok over medium heat. Add the garlic and cook for 1 minute. Add the prosciutto, oregano and prawns and cook for a further 1–2 minutes or until the prawns are tender and no longer translucent.

Add pasta to the hot pan and toss together quickly. Serve immediately with cracked black pepper.

ALTERNATIVES
mussels, clams, pipis, calamari (squid), cuttlefish, abalone

Preparing

Fish

To scale fish, hold the fish firmly by the tail, lifting slightly off the work surface. With a knife or fish scaler, scrape away the scales in the direction of the head. Repeat on other side and rinse.

Gut whole fish through the stomach. Slice the fish from the tail to the gills with a sharp knife. Remove the stomach contents and rinse thoroughly. Anything remaining will make the fish taste bitter.

To fillet round fish, cut diagonally with a sharp filleting knife just behind the gills until you reach the backbone. With the knife at an angle against the backbone, carefully slide towards the tail. At the tail, turn the knife blade up and cut the fillet. Repeat on other side.

To fillet flat fish, cut around the edges of the fish to outline the fillet shape. Cut into the flesh along the backbone and slice along the top of the ribs towards the edge, then from the head to the tail. Repeat on the other side of the backbone. Turn the fish over and repeat.

Another way to fillet a whole fish is to take the bone out. The result is one complete fillet. The head and tail can be left intact to hold the fish together while cooking. After gutting and trimming, slice the stomach as far as the tail. Hold the fish open and snip the backbone at the tail end with a pair of kitchen scissors. If leaving the head intact, snip the backbone at that end. Gently pull out the backbone. Remove the ribs with a knife, cutting just under the rib cage. Rinse under cold running water.

To skin a fish, first cut the fish into fillets. Lay the fillet, skin side down, on a board. Hold the tail end firmly between your fingers (salt will help you grip) and slice between the flesh and skin. With the knife at a slight angle, cut away from you with a smooth stroke.

Shellfish

To peel prawns, twist the head away from the body. Remove the shell; leave the tail intact if desired. Run a sharp knife down the back of the prawn and remove the vein. Green (raw) prawns are best prepared under cold running water.

Rinse crabs then open the body by twisting off the apron flap (tail). Insert your thumb or a knife under the top shell from the back. Prise off the shell.

fish&shellfish

Remove the guts and gills under cold running water. Cut the body in half or quarters. Twist off legs and claws and crack open with a nutcracker or with the back of a heavy knife. Remove the meat with a crab pick or skewer.

For lobsters and bugs, place the green (raw) or cooked shellfish on a flat surface, stomach side down. Insert a large knife through the centre of the body and cut all the way through the body towards the tail. Turn over and cut in the centre of the body towards the head. Gently pull apart and rinse under cold running water. Legs and claws can be twisted off and cracked with a nutcracker or the back of a heavy knife. Remove the rest of the meat from the body. It is easier to remove meat from cooked shellfish. Use kitchen scissors for raw shellfish.

Oysters bought alive in the shell need shucking. To shuck, lay the oyster with the flat shell up. Insert an oyster knife between the two shells, twist and prise open the shell. Remove the muscle attached to the top shell and discard.

Mussels, pipis and clams will need a thorough scrub under cold running water. Remove the stringy beard from mussels by pulling out sharply. Pipis and clams should be soaked in cold water for up to one hour to remove any sand.

Rinse octopus, cuttlefish and squid under cold running water before preparing. With octopus, make a small cut at the base of the head, remove the intestines and discard. Wash the inside of the head. Remove the hard beak (mouth) in the centre of the arms and discard. Rinse and cut into segments.

With cuttlefish and squid, remove the head and tentacles from the hood (body). Cut off tentacles and discard the head. Remove the quill or cartilage bone and discard. Pull the skin off the body and fins and discard the skin. Remove the ink sac attached to the head (the ink can be used for sauces). If the sac breaks, wash with water.

For abalone, remove the flesh from the shell by sliding a small knife around the edge between the flesh and the shell. Pull the flesh from the shell. Slice the intestines from the shell and discard. Trim off the dark portions. Abalone should be tenderised before cooking. Cut into two 5 mm (1/8 in) slices, cover with strong plastic and beat with a wooden mallet until limp.

53

SERVES 4 AS A MAIN

PREPARATION TIME: 25 minutes

WINE STYLE: medium-dry riesling

Prawns in a Coconut Curry Sauce

2 tablespoons butter

1 medium-sized onion, finely chopped

1 clove garlic, finely chopped

1 tablespoon grated ginger

1 tablespoon red curry paste (see page 159)

4 kaffir lime leaves, finely shredded (see page 158)

500 ml (2 cups) coconut milk

1 kg (2 lb) green (raw) bay prawns, peeled and deveined

1/3 cup chopped coriander leaves

Heat the butter in a frying pan over medium heat. Add the onion, garlic and ginger and cook until softened. Add the curry paste and lime leaves and stir for 1 minute. Add the coconut milk and simmer until the sauce reduces and thickens slightly.

Add the prawns and stir in the coriander. Cook for 2–3 minutes or until the prawns are tender and no longer translucent.

Transfer to warm serving bowls and serve with steamed jasmine rice.

ALTERNATIVES
cuttlefish, calamari (squid), crabs, bugs

SERVES 4 AS A STARTER
PREPARATION TIME: 15 minutes
WINE STYLE: medium-bodied chardonnay

Seared Scallops with Daikon Salad

3 tablespoons sesame oil

3 tablespoons rice vinegar

1 tablespoon sugar

2 tablespoons soy sauce

1 large daikon, julienned
(see page 157)

1 medium-sized carrot, julienned

1 tablespoon olive oil

12 large scallops, cleaned

1 tablespoon black sesame seeds
(see page 156)

Place the sesame oil, rice vinegar, sugar and soy sauce in a small bowl and mix together. Add the daikon and carrot and toss together. Set aside.

Heat the olive oil in a frying pan over high heat. Add the scallops and sear for 15–20 seconds on each side or until just cooked.

To serve, divide the salad between four serving plates, top with the scallops and sprinkle with black sesame seeds.

ALTERNATIVES

prawns, calamari (squid), cuttlefish, abalone

SERVES 4 AS A STARTER
PREPARATION TIME: 20 minutes
WINE STYLE: dry viognier

Stir-fried Squid with Shiitake & Bok Choy

2 tablespoons grapeseed oil

4 heads bok choy, halved

2 cloves garlic, finely chopped

2 tablespoons grated ginger

2 tablespoons light soy sauce

1 tablespoon mirin (see page 159)

6 large shiitake mushrooms, finely sliced (see page 159)

500 g (1 lb) squid, cleaned and cut into strips

Heat the grapeseed oil in a wok over high heat. Add the bok choy, garlic, ginger, soy sauce and mirin. Stir-fry for 1 minute.

Add the mushrooms and squid and stir-fry for a further 2 minutes or until the squid is no longer translucent and is just cooked.

To serve, divide between four small serving plates and spoon steamed rice to the side.

ALTERNATIVES
prawns, cuttlefish, scallops, baby octopus

57

SERVES 4 AS A STARTER
PREPARATION TIME: 15 minutes
WINE STYLE: medium-dry riesling

Stir-fried Abalone with Chinese Greens

1 small bunch bok choy, chopped into 3 cm (1¼ in) lengths

1 small bunch choy sum, chopped into 3 cm (1¼ in) lengths

1 tablespoon sesame oil

1 tablespoon olive oil

1 clove garlic, finely chopped

1 teaspoon grated ginger

3 tablespoons light soy sauce

3 tablespoons Chinese rice wine

½ cup cashews, toasted (see page 160)

250 g (8 oz) abalone meat, thinly sliced

Blanch bok choy and choy sum in boiling water for 30 seconds. Drain and set aside.

Heat the oils in a wok over high heat. Add the garlic and ginger and cook for 1 minute. Add the soy sauce, rice wine, cashews and abalone and stir-fry for 30 seconds. Add the bok choy and choy sum, toss to coat and serve immediately.

ALTERNATIVES
cuttlefish, calamari (squid), baby octopus, prawns

SERVES 4 AS A STARTER
PREPARATION TIME: 15 minutes
WINE STYLE: full-bodied dry gewurztraminer

Thai Cuttlefish Salad

2 tablespoons peanut oil

8 spring onions, trimmed and sliced

1 tablespoon grated ginger

2 small red chillies, finely chopped

16 medium-sized snowpeas, trimmed

2 large tomatoes, chopped

1 large cucumber, sliced

3 tablespoons soy sauce

1 tablespoon fish sauce

1 tablespoon brown sugar

1/3 cup coriander leaves

1 kg (2 lb) cuttlefish, cleaned and sliced

2 tablespoons lime juice

Heat the oil in a wok over high heat. Add the spring onions, ginger and chilli. Stir-fry for 2 minutes. Add the snowpeas, tomatoes, cucumber, soy sauce, fish sauce and sugar and cook for 1 minute. Add the coriander and cuttlefish and stir-fry for 2 minutes or until the cuttlefish is tender. Toss through the lime juice and serve immediately with steamed jasmine rice.

ALTERNATIVES
calamari (squid), scampi (meat only), bugs (meat only), scallop meat

Yabbies Fried in Orange & Basil

2 tablespoons olive oil
1 large Spanish onion, chopped
juice of 1 large orange
1 tablespoon orange zest
2 tablespoons chopped basil leaves
12 small yabbies, halved lengthwise
cracked black pepper

Heat the oil in a frying pan over medium to high heat. Add the onions and sauté for 2 minutes or until softened. Add the orange juice and zest and cook for 3 minutes. Add the basil and yabbies, and cook for 3 minutes or until the yabbies change colour and are cooked through. Remove from the frying pan with tongs and place on a serving platter. Pour over the sauce and sprinkle with cracked black pepper.

ALTERNATIVES
scampi, bugs, prawns, marron, scallops

Warm Salad of Bay Prawns & Broad Beans

SERVES 4 AS A MAIN

PREPARATION TIME: 15 minutes

WINE STYLE: medium-bodied chardonnay

400 g (14 oz) fresh broad beans, shelled

4 tablespoons olive oil

1 large onion, finely chopped

2 cloves garlic, finely chopped

750 g (1½ lb) medium-sized green (raw) bay prawns, peeled and deveined

1 small lemon, halved

sea salt

cracked black pepper

Place the broad beans in a saucepan of boiling water and cook for 5–6 minutes or until just tender. Drain and set aside.

Heat the oil in a frying pan over medium heat. Add the onion and garlic and cook until softened. Add prawns and cook until they are no longer translucent. Remove from the heat and toss through the broad beans.

Garnish with a squeeze of lemon juice, sea salt and cracked black pepper.

ALTERNATIVES
scallops, calamari (squid), mussels, abalone

61

SERVES 4 AS A STARTER

PREPARATION TIME: 25 minutes

WINE STYLE: medium-dry gewurztraminer

King Prawn Rice Paper Rolls

60 ml (¼ cup) peanut oil

12 large green (raw) king prawns, shelled and deveined

100 g (3 oz) rice vermicelli noodles

12 round rice paper wrappers (see page 159)

3 large lettuce leaves, washed, cut lengthwise

12 mint leaves

½ cup coriander leaves

½ cup bean sprouts

½ cup shredded carrot

12 stalks garlic chives or chives

DIPPING SAUCE

2 tablespoons sweet chilli sauce

1 tablespoon fish sauce

1 tablespoon lime juice

2 tablespoons water

Heat the oil in a frying pan over medium heat. Add the prawns and sauté for 2 minutes, or until they just turn pink. Remove and set aside.

Soak the rice vermicelli in hot water until soft. Drain well and set aside.

Soak three rice papers at a time in warm water until soft. Transfer to a flat dry surface. Place a small amount of the rice vermicelli noodles onto each rice paper and top each with 1 prawn. Add small amounts of lettuce, 1 mint leaf, coriander, bean sprouts, carrot and garlic chives to each rice paper. Fold over and roll up to secure. Repeat for the remaining rolls.

For the dipping sauce, combine the chilli sauce, fish sauce, lime juice and water.

Serve the rolls with a small bowl of dipping sauce.

ALTERNATIVES

bugs, calamari (squid), crab, oysters, mussels

Dory Fillets with Apple & Cucumber Salsa

SALSA

2 tablespoons olive oil

1 medium-sized
Spanish onion, finely diced

2 small tomatoes, finely diced

2 small green apples, peeled and diced

2 small Lebanese cucumbers,
peeled and diced

1 tablespoon chopped thyme leaves

3 tablespoons chopped chervil leaves

2 tablespoons lime juice

2 john dory fillets
(about 200 g/7 oz each), trimmed

olive oil for frying

For the salsa, heat the olive oil over medium heat in a frying pan. Add the onion and sauté for 1–2 minutes. Add tomato, apple, cucumber, thyme and half the chervil. Cook for 1 minute. Remove from the heat and transfer the salsa mixture to a bowl. Spoon over the lime juice and set aside.

Return the frying pan to the heat, add a little olive oil and pan-fry the fillets until slightly golden, about 2 minutes each side.

To serve, place the fillets on serving plates and top with salsa and the remaining chervil.

ALTERNATIVES
any type of dory fillets, morwong, trevally, sea perch, snapper, whiting, flounder

63

Roasting & Baking

Baby Barramundi filled with Bok Choy & Macadamia Nuts

Baked Murray Cod with Wild Rice & Pinenut Stuffing

Baked Ocean Trout with Spinach & Almond Stuffing

Baked Snapper with Buckwheat & Shiitake Stuffing

Barramundi Fillets with Fennel, Capers & Olives

Red Emperor with Steamed Greens & Saffron Hollandaise

Blue Eye Cutlets with Sage & Garlic Potatoes

Bream Fillets Baked in Paper with Ginger & Lime

Lime-roasted Morwong with Snake Beans

Prosciutto-wrapped Ling with Melon & Mint Salsa

Pastry-baked Mullet with Tomato & Herb Filling

Trevally Fillets with Herb Crust

Blue Grenadier Baked in Chermoula

Rosemary-baked Orange Roughy

Shredded Tuna Salad with Spring Onion & Chilli

Soy & Sesame Sweet-lip Emperor with Sautéed Beans

Whiting Braised in White Wine & Tarragon

Whole Dory with White Wine & Mushrooms

Roasting

ROASTING AND BAKING are simple and effective methods for cooking seafood. Roasting is usually done with the seafood uncovered in an oven between 180°C and 220°C, whereas baking involves covering seafood and cooking at temperatures between 140°C and 230°C.

Roasting and baking can give the outside of seafood a crispy, golden coating while retaining the moisture inside. Both methods are suited to almost all whole fish, cutlets and fillets.

Equipment

An oven and a suitable baking pan or dish.

A kettle barbecue.

How to roast and bake

Score a whole fish to allow it to cook evenly. Do this by making two or three diagonal cuts across the thickest parts of both sides of the body.

Place the seafood in a single layer in an oiled baking dish and baste with oil, butter or marinade. Oily fish can be basted with a citrus marinade, as most oil is stored under the skin. Fillets should be placed skin side up to protect the flesh.

Always cook seafood in a preheated oven, and baste the seafood at regular intervals during cooking.

Baking

Baby Barramundi filled with Bok Choy & Macadamia Nuts

SERVES 4 AS A MAIN
PREPARATION TIME: 1 hour
WINE STYLE: full-bodied chardonnay

4 large heads bok choy, chopped

80 ml (1/3 cup) olive oil

4 tablespoons soy sauce

3 medium-sized spring onions, chopped

2 cloves garlic, finely chopped

2/3 cup macadamia nuts, coarsely chopped

4 small whole baby barramundi (about 300 g/10 oz each), cleaned

olive oil for basting

sea salt and white pepper

60 ml (1/4 cup) water

juice of 1 small lime

Preheat the oven to 180°C.

For the filling, combine the bok choy, oil, soy sauce, spring onions, garlic and macadamia nuts. Set aside.

Fill the cavity of each barramundi with the mixture. Secure with a bamboo skewer or toothpicks. Brush the outside of each fish generously with olive oil and season with sea salt and white pepper. Place in a shallow baking dish and pour in the water and lime juice. Cover with aluminium foil and bake for 20–25 minutes or until the flesh flakes. Baste frequently, and add more water if necessary.

When done, remove the fish from the baking dish, reserving the juices. Place each fish on a serving plate and spoon over a little of the juice.

ALTERNATIVES
red mullet, sand whiting, snapper, morwong, coral trout, rainbow trout

Baked Murray Cod with Wild Rice & Pinenut Stuffing

SERVES 4 AS A MAIN

PREPARATION TIME: 55 minutes

WINE STYLE: medium-bodied pinot noir

1/3 cup wild rice

1/3 cup long-grain rice

2 tablespoons olive oil

1/3 cup pinenuts

3 spring onions, chopped

1 teaspoon lemon zest

1 tablespoon capers, chopped

20 baby spinach leaves, chopped

sea salt and black pepper

1 whole Murray cod
(about 1.2 kg/2 lb), cleaned

olive oil for basting

For the stuffing, cook the wild rice and long-grain rice separately until tender. Drain and set aside.

Preheat the oven to 180°C.

Heat the olive oil in a frying pan over medium heat. Add the pinenuts and cook until golden. Add the spring onions, lemon zest and capers and cook for a further 2 minutes, or until softened.

In a bowl, combine the cooked rice, nut mixture and spinach leaves. Season with salt and pepper.

Spoon the stuffing into the cavity of the fish and secure with toothpicks or a skewer. Brush the body of the fish generously with oil and place on a shallow baking tray. Bake for 30 minutes or until the flesh flakes when tested with a fork.

To serve, place the fish on a large serving platter and surround with steamed green vegetables.

ALTERNATIVES
snapper, silver perch, coral trout, ocean trout, jewfish, barramundi, emperor

Baked Ocean Trout with Spinach & Almond Stuffing

SERVES 4 AS A MAIN

PREPARATION TIME: 1 hour

WINE STYLE: full-bodied chardonnay

2 tablespoons unsalted butter

1 small onion, chopped

2 cloves garlic, finely chopped

3 tablespoons chopped lemon thyme leaves

3 cups chopped spinach

1/4 cup almond slivers, chopped

1/2 cup fresh breadcrumbs

1 large ocean trout (about 2 kg/4 lb), cleaned and backbone removed*

olive oil for basting

salt and pepper

* ask your fishmonger to do this for you

Preheat the oven to 180°C.

To prepare the stuffing, melt the butter in a frying pan over medium heat. Add the onion and garlic and sauté for 2 minutes or until softened. Add the lemon thyme and spinach and sauté for 1 minute. Remove from the heat and place the mixture in a mixing bowl. Add the almonds and breadcrumbs to the mixture and combine. Set aside until ready to use.

Place the trout on a flat surface and fill the cavity with the stuffing. Secure with bamboo skewers or toothpicks.

Place the fish in a large roasting pan and brush all over with olive oil. Season with salt and pepper and cover with aluminium foil. Bake for 40 minutes, or until the fish is cooked through and the flesh flakes when tested with a fork.

To serve, place the fish on a large platter and remove the skewers.

ALTERNATIVES
red mullet, snapper, baby barramundi, whiting

Baked Snapper with Buckwheat & Shiitake Stuffing

SERVES 4 AS A MAIN
PREPARATION TIME: 1 hour 10 minutes
WINE STYLE: light-bodied pinot noir

2 tablespoons butter

1 cup buckwheat, whole

500 ml (2 cups) water or chicken stock (see page 157)

1 large onion, finely chopped

2 rashers bacon, finely chopped

150 g (5 oz) shiitake mushrooms, finely sliced (see page 160)

2 tablespoons finely chopped tarragon

1 whole snapper (about 1.5 kg/3 lb), cleaned and backbone removed*

olive oil for basting

* ask your fishmonger to do this for you

Preheat the oven to 180°C.

Melt 1 tablespoon of the butter in a large frying pan over medium heat, add the buckwheat and coat with butter. Pour in the boiling water or stock, cover and simmer for 10 minutes. Remove from the heat and place the buckwheat in a large mixing bowl.

Return the frying pan to the heat and melt the remaining butter. Add the onion and bacon and sauté until the onion is soft. Add the mushrooms and sauté until tender. Remove from the heat and add to the buckwheat. Add the tarragon and combine thoroughly.

Spoon the buckwheat mixture into the cavity of the fish, pushing well down into the stomach. Secure with toothpicks, or loosely stitch with a needle and thread.

Brush the fish all over with olive oil, place on a baking tray and bake for 30–35 minutes, or until the fish is cooked through.

Remove from the oven and rest for 10 minutes in a warm place.

Serve the snapper on a large platter with steamed greens.

ALTERNATIVES
Atlantic salmon, ocean trout, coral trout, emperor, Murray cod, silver perch

Barramundi Fillets with Fennel, Capers & Olives

SERVES 4 AS A MAIN
PREPARATION TIME: 35 minutes
WINE STYLE: dry rosé

**4 barramundi fillets
(about 200 g/7 oz each)**

80 ml (1/3 cup) olive oil

sea salt and freshly ground pepper

1 large fennel bulb, trimmed and sliced

**12 medium-sized kalamata olives,
pitted and chopped**

**1 tablespoon capers,
drained and chopped**

1 tablespoon lemon juice

Preheat the oven to 180°C.

Trim the fillets and slice each in half crosswise. Brush each piece of fish with a little olive oil and season with salt and pepper. Place on a baking tray and roast for 10–12 minutes, or until the fish is soft to the touch.

Meanwhile, in a frying pan heat the remaining olive oil over medium heat. Add the fennel, olives, capers and lemon juice. Cook for 4–5 minutes or until the fennel is soft.

Remove from the heat and spoon the fennel mixture onto warm serving plates. Top with the fillets and serve immediately.

ALTERNATIVES
sea perch, Atlantic salmon, ocean trout, blue eye, gemfish

71

Red Emperor with Steamed Greens & Saffron Hollandaise

SERVES 4 AS A MAIN

PREPARATION TIME: 50 minutes

WINE STYLE: full-bodied chardonnay

1 large red emperor
(about 2 kg/4 lb), cleaned and scaled

375 ml (1½ cups) dry white wine

4 large bay leaves

3 large zucchini, sliced lengthwise

2 bunches asparagus,
trimmed and halved

3 large egg yolks

1 teaspoon saffron threads,
soaked in 2 tablespoons water

225 g (7½ oz) unsalted butter, melted

juice of ½ small lemon

salt and white pepper

Preheat the oven to 180°C.

Place the fish on a flat surface and make two or three diagonal slits on both sides of the fish. Place the fish in a large roasting pan, pour in the wine and scatter bay leaves around. Baste with the liquid, cover tightly with aluminium foil and bake for 35–40 minutes or until cooked through. Set aside in a warm place for 10 minutes.

Bring a saucepan of water to the boil and cover with a bamboo steamer. Place the zucchini and asparagus inside the steamer. Cover and steam until tender.

Meanwhile, place the egg yolks and saffron liquid in a saucepan and whisk together until frothy. Place the saucepan over low heat and whisk continuously for 5 minutes, or until the mixture has thickened. Remove from the heat and pour in the melted butter, whisking until thickened. Whisk in the lemon juice, salt and pepper.

To serve, place the fish on a large platter surrounded with zucchini and asparagus. Drizzle with the saffron hollandaise and serve immediately.

ALTERNATIVES
snapper, baby jewfish, ocean trout, barramundi, morwong, coral trout

Blue Eye Cutlets with Sage & Garlic Potatoes

SERVES 4 AS A MAIN
PREPARATION TIME: 45 minutes
WINE STYLE: full-bodied chardonnay

4 large potatoes, thinly sliced

12 sage leaves, chopped

3 cloves garlic, finely chopped

olive oil

4 blue eye cutlets
(about 200 g/7 oz each)

2 tablespoons olive oil

cracked black pepper

1 bunch baby rocket, trimmed

Preheat the oven to 200°C.

Arrange the potato slices on a baking tray and sprinkle with sage and garlic. Drizzle with olive oil and bake for 30 minutes or until the potatoes are soft.

Meanwhile, brush the cutlets with olive oil and season with cracked black pepper. Place the cutlets on a baking tray lined with non-stick paper and bake for 10–12 minutes, or until the cutlets are just cooked through.

Place the potatoes on serving plates and top with the cutlets and rocket leaves.

ALTERNATIVES
jewfish, gemfish, Atlantic salmon, ocean trout, kingfish

Bream Fillets Baked in Paper with Ginger & Lime

SERVES 4 AS A MAIN

PREPARATION TIME: 25 minutes

WINE STYLE: medium-dry riesling

4 sheets non-stick baking paper, cut into 25 cm (10 in) squares

4 bream fillets (about 200 g/7 oz each), trimmed

4 kaffir lime leaves, shredded (see page 158)

2 stalks spring onions, sliced finely

4 tablespoons grapeseed oil

2 tablespoons soy sauce

1 tablespoon grated ginger

2 tablespoons lime juice

4 tablespoons coriander leaves

lime wedges

Preheat the oven to 180°C.

Place each fillet on a small sheet of baking paper. Fold up the edges of the paper around the fillets to hold in the sauce. Top each fillet with lime leaves and spring onions.

In a bowl, combine the oil, soy sauce, ginger and lime juice. Spoon the sauce into the parcels and top with coriander leaves. Secure each parcel by double-folding the baking paper. Place on a baking tray and bake for 10 minutes or until the fish is opaque and is just cooked through. Serve with additional lime wedges.

ALTERNATIVES
blue eye, flathead, ling, boneless fillets, Atlantic salmon, ocean trout

PREPARATION TIME: 45 minutes

WINE STYLE: sauvignon blanc

Lime-roasted Morwong with Snake Beans

2 tablespoons lime zest

juice of 2 large limes

2 cloves garlic, finely chopped

2 teaspoons sugar

125 ml (1/2 cup) olive oil

3 tablespoons finely chopped coriander

1 large morwong
(about 1.5 kg/3 lb), cleaned

2 tablespoons butter

1 tablespoon light soy sauce

400 g (14 oz) snake beans, halved

In a bowl, combine the lime zest and juice, garlic, sugar, oil and coriander. Set aside.

With a sharp knife, make 2 or 3 diagonal slits on both sides of the fish. Place the fish in a large dish and pour over the marinade. Cover and refrigerate for 1 hour or until ready to cook.

Preheat the oven to 180°C.

Remove the fish from the marinade and place on a large baking tray. Baste generously with the marinade, cover with aluminium foil and cook for 15 minutes. Remove the foil and baste with the remaining marinade. Cook for a further 10–15 minutes or until the fish is cooked through.

Meanwhile, melt the butter in a frying pan or wok over medium heat, add the soy sauce and snake beans and stir-fry until tender.

To serve, place the whole fish on a large serving platter. Surround with the snake beans.

ALTERNATIVES
snapper, Murray cod, silver perch, barramundi, coral trout, emperor

Prosciutto-wrapped Ling with Melon & Mint Salsa

4 ling fillets
(about 200 g/7 oz each), trimmed

white pepper

12 slices prosciutto

2 tablespoons unsalted butter

SALSA

½ medium-sized
honeydew melon, cut into small dice

1 small cucumber, seeded and diced

2 medium-sized tomatoes,
cut into small dice

2 tablespoons finely
chopped mint leaves

1 tablespoon finely chopped parsley

1 tablespoon balsamic vinegar

2 tablespoons olive oil

a pinch each of salt and white pepper

Cut and trim each fillet into 2 square shapes. Place the fillets on a flat, dry surface and season with pepper. Wrap three slices of prosciutto around each portion of ling, securing with string (or toothpicks). Set aside.

Preheat the oven to 180°C.

Melt the butter in a frying pan over high heat, add the fish and cook for 1–2 minutes on each side or until golden. Place on a baking tray lined with non-stick baking paper. Bake for 6–8 minutes or until the ling is just cooked through.

Meanwhile, in a bowl combine the melon, cucumber, tomato, mint and parsley. Add the balsamic vinegar, oil, salt and pepper. Toss together gently.

Place the fish on warm serving plates and serve with the melon salsa on the side.

ALTERNATIVES
gemfish, blue eye, boneless fillets, Atlantic salmon, ocean trout

Pastry-baked Mullet with Tomato & Herb Filling

SERVES 4 AS A MAIN
PREPARATION TIME: 1 hour 10 minutes
WINE STYLE: unoaked semillon

1 medium-sized mullet (about 1 kg/2 lb), cleaned

2 tablespoons olive oil

1 medium-sized onion, finely chopped

3 cloves garlic, finely chopped

1 medium-sized red capsicum, seeded and sliced

3 medium-sized tomatoes, chopped

3 tablespoons chopped basil

1 tablespoon chopped oregano

salt and pepper

2 ready-rolled puff pastry sheets

1 large egg yolk, beaten

Remove the head and carefully remove the backbone of the fish by cutting along either side of the bone. Remove any other bones. Snip off the fins and leave the tail intact. (You can ask your fishmonger to do this for you.) Rinse the fish well, cover and refrigerate until ready to cook.

Heat the oil in a frying pan over medium heat. Add the onion, garlic and capsicum and sauté until softened. Add the tomatoes, basil and oregano and sauté for 1–2 minutes or until softened. Season to taste with salt and pepper. Remove from the heat.

Preheat the oven to 180°C.

Place the fish on a flat dry surface and fill the cavity with the tomato mixture, packing firmly. Place the fish in the centre of the pastry. Fold one side of the pastry up and over the fish and brush the top of the pastry with the egg yolk. Fold over the other side of the pastry and press together gently to seal. Turn the fish over, sealed side down, and glaze with the remaining egg yolk. Decorate with the remaining pastry, if you wish. Make three small slashes across the top of the pastry so the steam can escape.

Place the fish on a baking tray and bake for 35–40 minutes or until golden brown.

Serve the baked mullet on a large serving plate with roasted vegetables.

ALTERNATIVES
morwong, silver bream, barramundi, snapper

SERVES 4 AS A MAIN

PREPARATION TIME: 20 minutes

WINE STYLE: light-bodied pinot noir

Trevally Fillets
with Herb Crust

**4 trevally fillets
(about 150 g / 5 oz), trimmed**

salt and pepper

4 tablespoons unsalted butter, softened

1½ cups fresh breadcrumbs

¼ cup grated parmesan cheese

2 cloves garlic, finely chopped

2 tablespoons chopped parsley

2 tablespoons chopped basil

200 g (7 oz) baby English spinach, washed

lemon wedges to serve

Preheat the oven to 170°C.

Place the fillets on a baking tray lined with non-stick baking paper. Season with salt and pepper.

In a mixing bowl combine the butter, breadcrumbs, parmesan, garlic, parsley and basil. Spread the mixture evenly over the top of each fillet.

Place the tray in an oven and bake for 10 minutes or until the fish is just cooked and the crust is golden.

Arrange the spinach leaves on serving plates and top with the fillets. Serve immediately with lemon wedges.

ALTERNATIVES
sardines (pilchards), mullet, morwong, tuna, swordfish

SERVES 4 AS A MAIN
PREPARATION TIME: 40 minutes
WINE STYLE: medium-dry riesling

Blue Grenadier
Baked in Chermoula

CHERMOULA

$1/3$ cup coriander leaves

$1/3$ cup parsley leaves

3 cloves garlic

2 teaspoons sweet paprika

2 teaspoons ground cumin

125 ml ($1/2$ cup) olive oil

3 tablespoons lemon juice

4 blue grenadier fillets
(about 200 g/7 oz each)

125 ml ($1/2$ cup) water

2 cups couscous

boiling water

1 tablespoon butter

Preheat the oven to 200°C.

For the chermoula, place the coriander, parsley, garlic, paprika, cumin, oil and lemon juice in a food processor. Process until smooth.

Pour the chermoula into a baking dish, add the fillets and coat well. Add the water and cover the baking dish with aluminium foil. Bake for 25 minutes, remove from the oven and baste generously with the sauce. Reduce the oven temperature to 180°C and bake for a further 5–10 minutes, or until the fillets are opaque and flake easily when tested.

Meanwhile, place the couscous in a large bowl and pour in enough boiling water to cover the couscous. Add the butter and set aside for 5 minutes to allow the water to absorb.

Place the fillets on serving plates, top with the remaining sauce and spoon couscous to the side.

ALTERNATIVES
sea perch, blue eye, ling, gemfish, snapper, emperor, Atlantic salmon, ocean trout

81

Rosemary-baked Orange Roughy

1 tablespoon olive oil

1 small onion, finely chopped

2 cloves garlic, finely chopped

2 tablespoons chopped rosemary leaves

1 tablespoon orange zest

125 ml ($\frac{1}{2}$ cup) lemon juice

125 ml ($\frac{1}{2}$ cup) orange juice

125 ml ($\frac{1}{2}$ cup) white wine

1 tablespoon light soy sauce

cracked black pepper

4 large orange roughy fillets
(about 175 g/6 oz each), trimmed

1 bunch rocket, stems removed

Heat the oil in a saucepan over medium heat. Add the onion and garlic and sauté for 1 minute or until softened. Add the rosemary and orange zest and combine well. Pour in the lemon juice, orange juice, wine and soy sauce. Add the black pepper and slowly bring to the boil.

Remove from the heat and allow to cool completely before use.

Place the fillets in a dish and pour over the cooled marinade. Cover and marinate for 30 minutes. (You can refrigerate for up to 3 hours if preparing in advance.)

Preheat the oven to 170°C.

Remove the fillets from the marinade and place on a baking tray lined with baking paper. Bake for 8–10 minutes or until the fillets are just cooked.

Return the reserved marinade to the saucepan and boil until the sauce becomes thick and syrupy. Remove from the heat and keep warm until the fish is done.

Place the fillets on serving plates and pour over a little of the sauce. Serve with rocket.

ALTERNATIVES
blue eye, barramundi, ling, gemfish, boneless fillets

SERVES 4 AS A STARTER
PREPARATION TIME: 20 minutes
WINE STYLE: full-bodied, dry rosé

Shredded Tuna Salad with Spring Onion & Chilli

4 tuna fillets (about 200 g / 7 oz each)

olive oil for basting

salt and pepper

**4 spring onions,
green part only, thinly sliced**

2 tablespoons olive oil

1 tablespoon soy sauce

juice of 2 small limes

**2 small red chillies, seeded
and finely chopped**

1/3 cup chopped coriander leaves

Preheat the oven to 180°C.

Brush the tuna fillets with oil and season with salt and pepper. Place on a baking tray and bake for 8–10 minutes or until the tuna is cooked through. Remove from the oven and set aside.

In a bowl, combine the spring onions, oil, soy sauce, lime juice and chillies. Set aside.

With clean hands, flake the fish into small pieces and add to the dressing. Combine thoroughly.

Divide the tuna salad between 4 serving plates. To serve, scatter with coriander leaves.

ALTERNATIVES
swordfish, marlin, ling, gemfish

Soy & Sesame Sweet-lip Emperor with Sautéed Beans

SERVES 4 AS A MAIN

PREPARATION TIME: 1 hour 10 minutes

WINE STYLE: medium-dry riesling

1 medium-sized sweet-lip emperor (about 1 kg / 2 lb), cleaned

80 ml (⅓ cup) light soy sauce

60 ml (¼ cup) mirin (see page 159)

3 tablespoons sesame oil

1 tablespoon brown sugar

1 clove garlic, finely chopped

2 spring onions, chopped

300 g (10 oz) green beans, trimmed

1 tablespoon black sesame seeds (see page 156)

Using a sharp knife, make 2 or 3 deep slits on both sides of the fish. Set aside. Place the fish on a large sheet of aluminium foil, folding up the sides to hold in the marinade.

In a bowl, combine the soy sauce, mirin, sesame oil, brown sugar and garlic. Pour three-quarters of the marinade over the fish and sprinkle the spring onions on top. Fold over the foil to form a large parcel. Place on a baking tray and set aside to marinate for 30 minutes.

Preheat the oven to 180°C.

Steam the fish in the oven for 20–25 minutes or until just cooked through.

Heat the remaining marinade in a wok, add beans and black sesame seeds and sauté until the beans are tender.

Place the fish on a large platter surrounded by sautéed beans and serve with steamed rice.

ALTERNATIVES
snapper, barramundi, leatherjacket, silver bream, coral trout, silver perch, Murray cod, red mullet

Whiting Braised in White Wine & Tarragon

8 small whiting fillets
(about 100 g/3½ oz each), trimmed
100g (3½ oz) butter
500 ml (2 cups) white wine
1 tablespoon finely chopped tarragon
salt and pepper
1 tablespoon chopped chives

Preheat the oven to 180°C.

Place the fish in a greased baking dish.

Melt the butter in a saucepan over medium heat. Add the white wine, tarragon, salt and pepper. Simmer and reduce the liquid by half. Pour the liquid over the fillets and bake for 8–10 minutes or until the fish is just cooked.

To serve, place the fillets on serving plates and spoon over a little of the liquid. Sprinkle with chives.

ALTERNATIVES
dory, snapper, rainbow trout, garfish

Whole Dory with White Wine & Mushrooms

4 small john dory, whole, cleaned
750 ml (3 cups) dry white wine
125 g (4 oz) butter
1 small onion, finely chopped
12 small mushrooms, sliced
60 ml (¼ cup) lemon juice
80 ml (⅓ cup) cream
2 tablespoons chervil leaves
lemon wedges to serve

Preheat the oven to 180°C.

Trim the top and bottom fins of the fish with a pair of kitchen scissors. Gently make two diagonal slits across the thickest part of the fish, making sure the slits are not too deep. Place in a large baking dish (you may need two).

Add 250 ml (1 cup) of wine per baking dish and dot each fish with 1 tablespoon of butter. Cover with aluminium foil and bake for 8–10 minutes or until the fish is just cooked through.

Meanwhile, in a frying pan add the remaining butter and melt over medium heat. Add the onion and sauté until golden. Add the mushrooms and cook for 2 minutes or until softened. Add the remaining wine, lemon juice and cream and cook for a further 2 minutes.

To serve, place the fish on serving plates and spoon over the sauce. Garnish with chervil and lemon wedges.

ALTERNATIVES
snapper, flathead, morwong, whiting, flounder, rainbow trout

Barbecuing

& Grilling

Grilled Red Mullet with Tomato & Fennel

Chargrilled Perch with Fennel & Watercress Salad

Grilled Sardines with Haloumi & Tomato Salad

Garlic-grilled Warehou with Celery, Fennel & Pear Salad

Grilled Trout with Beetroot, Beans & Walnut Dressing

Grilled Skate with Black Bean Sauce & Asian Greens

Grilled Tandoori Ling with Cucumber & Mint Yoghurt

Grilled Tuna Steaks with Wasabi & Basil Butter

Coconut & Ginger Grilled Mackerel

Salt-grilled Salmon Skewers with Coriander & Mint Pesto

Snapper in Vine Leaves with Tomato & Bocconcini Salad

Peppered Sea Perch with Garlic Potatoes & Parsley Oil

Grilled Whole Flounder with Lemon & Thyme

Grilled Lobster with Salsa Verde

Grilled Prawn Skewers with Pernod Mayo

Lime-marinated Bugs

Crispy Barbecued Octopus

Oysters Kilpatrick

Sugarcane Prawns with Dipping Sauce

Sea Perch Fillets with Hot Tomato Broth

BBQing

BARBECUING AND GRILLING are dry heat methods in which the heat source comes from only one direction. Heating from above is done with a salamander or oven grill, and heating from below is done with a grill or chargrill.

Most whole fish and oily or moist fillets are suitable for barbecuing and grilling. For delicate fish, cover the grill with perforated aluminium foil to help prevent the fish drying out and falling apart when placed on intense heat. Any raw shellfish that is basted or marinated is great on the grill.

Equipment

Charcoal barbecue

Electric barbecue

Gas barbecue

Chargrill

Salamander or oven grill

Grilling

How to barbecue or grill

Marinating fish or shellfish before barbecuing or grilling enhances the flavour and protects the flesh from drying out.

Brush the grill with oil to prevent seafood from sticking. An electric grill should be set at a medium-high heat, whereas a gas grill should be set at a medium heat.

Whole fish should be scored with two or three diagonal cuts across the thickest parts of both sides of the fish. Leaving the head and tail intact retains moisture and flavour.

Turn whole fish and fillets only once, about halfway through the desired cooking time. Thin fillets may not need to be turned. Use oil, butter or marinade to baste the seafood as it cooks.

When making seafood skewers, push the pieces together so that the flavours blend and the flesh holds together.

SERVES 4 AS A MAIN

PREPARATION TIME: 25 minutes

WINE STYLE: unoaked sauvignon blanc

Grilled Red Mullet with Tomato & Fennel

4 medium-sized red mullet (about 200 g/7 oz each), cleaned and scaled

olive oil

salt and pepper

3 tablespoons olive oil

1 small onion, finely chopped

4 medium-sized tomatoes, chopped

1 small fennel bulb, finely chopped

juice of 1 large lemon

Place the red mullet on a flat surface and make 2 diagonal slits on both sides of the fish. Baste generously with oil and season with salt and pepper. Set aside.

Heat the 3 tablespoons of oil in a saucepan over medium heat. Add the onion and sauté until golden. Add the tomatoes, fennel and lemon juice and cook until softened. Season to taste with salt and pepper and remove from the heat. Set aside.

Preheat the grill to high.

Place the fish on the grill and cook for 3–4 minutes on each side or until cooked through.

To serve, place the fish on a large platter and spoon over the tomato and fennel sauce.

ALTERNATIVES
whiting, silver bream, garfish, pilchards, baby barramundi

Chargrilled Perch with Fennel & Watercress Salad

SERVES 4 AS A MAIN

PREPARATION TIME: 30 minutes

WINE STYLE: cool-climate sauvignon blanc

4 fennel bulbs, trimmed

1 bunch watercress, stems removed

4 tablespoons olive oil

2 tablespoons balsamic vinegar

a pinch of brown sugar

a pinch of white pepper

4 perch fillets
(about 200 g/7 oz each), trimmed

olive oil for basting

Cut the fennel in half and slice thinly. Place the fennel and watercress in a large bowl.

In another bowl, combine the oil, vinegar, sugar and pepper. Pour over the fennel and watercress and toss together gently. Set aside.

Brush the fillets with olive oil and place on a hot grill. Cook for 2 minutes on each side or until the fillets are golden and just cooked.

Place each fillet on a serving plate and serve with the fennel and watercress salad.

ALTERNATIVES
ocean perch, sea perch, snapper, blue eye, ocean trout, Atlantic salmon, ling, gemfish

Grilled Sardines with Haloumi & Tomato Salad

SERVES 4 AS A STARTER

PREPARATION TIME: 25 minutes

WINE STYLE: medium-bodied rosé

12 fresh sardines, cleaned and butterflied

salt and freshly ground pepper

1 clove garlic, finely chopped

1 tablespoon chopped thyme leaves

3 tablespoons chopped parsley

juice of 1 medium-sized lemon

125 ml (½ cup) olive oil

150 g (5 oz) haloumi, sliced (see page 158)

4 medium-sized roma tomatoes, quartered

Place the sardines on a flat surface and season with salt and pepper. Cover and refrigerate until ready to use.

In a bowl, combine the garlic, thyme, 1 tablespoon of the parsley, lemon juice and olive oil.

Preheat the grill to high.

Spoon half of the oil mixture over the sardines, making sure they are thoroughly coated.

Place the fish on the hot grill and cook for 2 minutes on each side or until golden. Set aside on a warm plate.

Brush the haloumi with oil and place on the hot grill and cook for 1 minute on each side. Transfer to a bowl, add the tomatoes and toss with the remaining olive oil mixture.

To serve, divide the haloumi and tomato between 4 serving plates, top with the grilled sardines and garnish with the remaining parsley.

ALTERNATIVES
blue mackerel, garfish, morwong, barramundi, whiting, mullet

Garlic-grilled Warehou with Celery, Fennel & Pear Salad

SERVES 4 AS A MAIN

PREPARATION TIME: 40 minutes

WINE STYLE: full-bodied semillon

4 medium-sized warehou fillets (about 150 g/5 oz each), trimmed

salt and pepper

60 ml (¼ cup) olive oil

3 cloves garlic, finely chopped

juice of 1 large lemon

1 small Spanish onion, sliced

4 stalks celery, sliced diagonally

1 large fennel bulb, trimmed and finely sliced

2 large ripe pears, quartered and sliced

1 large Lebanese cucumber, halved and sliced

2 tablespoons olive oil

2 tablespoons lemon juice, extra

Place the warehou fillets in a glass dish and season with salt and pepper. Combine the olive oil, garlic and lemon juice and pour over the fillets. Cover and refrigerate until ready to cook.

For the salad, combine the onion, celery, fennel, pear and cucumber. Add the oil and lemon juice and toss to combine.

Preheat the grill to high.

Remove the fillets from the marinade and place on the grill. Reserve the remaining marinade and use to baste the fish. Cook for 2 minutes on each side or until the fish is just cooked through.

To serve, place the grilled fillets on serving plates with the salad to the side.

ALTERNATIVES

morwong, barramundi, snapper, dory, whiting, flounder, Atlantic salmon, ocean trout

Grilled Trout with Beetroot, Beans & Walnut Dressing

SERVES 4 AS A MAIN
PREPARATION TIME: 40 minutes
WINE STYLE: medium-bodied pinot noir

12 small fresh beetroots, scrubbed

200 g (7 oz) green beans, trimmed

1/3 cup walnuts, chopped

1 1/2 tablespoons walnut oil

3 tablespoons olive oil

1 teaspoon Dijon mustard

salt and pepper

**4 trout fillets
(about 175 g/6 oz each), trimmed**

extra olive oil

Place the beetroots in a saucepan of boiling water and boil for 30 minutes or until tender. (A skewer should pierce the beetroot easily.) Remove beetroots from the saucepan and remove the skins by rubbing gently under running water. Set aside to cool before slicing.

Blanch the beans in boiling water, drain well and set aside to cool.

Slice the beetroot into small chunks and place in a large bowl. Add the beans and walnuts and toss together gently.

Combine the walnut oil, olive oil and mustard. Season with salt and pepper. Drizzle over the beetroot and beans and toss together gently. Set aside.

Brush the outside of the fish with oil and place on a hot grill for 2 minutes on each side or until just cooked.

To serve, place the fish on serving plates and with the beetroot salad on the side.

ALTERNATIVES
whiting, snapper, ocean perch, morwong, flounder, barramundi

Storing fish

Fish

To store whole fish, first wash the fish under cold running water. If the fish has been gutted, wash carefully inside the cavity and gently shake off any excess water. Place the fish on a plate, shallow dish or airtight container. Cover with cling film and refrigerate for 2–3 days.

With fillets, steaks or cutlets, remove the fish pieces from the plastic bag immediately and place on a plate, shallow dish or airtight container. Cover with cling film and refrigerate for 2–3 days.

Fish can be frozen, but some of the moisture and flavour will be lost. Freeze fish in the quantities to be used at one time. Wrap fish tightly in cling film and place inside a freezer bag. Fillets, cutlets and steaks should be wrapped in cling film individually and then placed in a freezer bag. Remove all the air from the freezer bag before sealing. It helps to label the freezer bag with a date. Fish can be frozen for up to 3 months. Thaw in the refrigerator.

Shellfish

To store prawns, leave them in their shells until ready to eat. This helps retain the moisture and flavour. Prawns can keep in the refrigerator for 2–3 days if stored in an airtight container.

For raw prawns, leave them in their shells until ready to cook. The heads can be removed before storing. Place the prawns in an airtight container with a little water and refrigerate for 1–2 days.

The best way to freeze prawns is in block form. Place prawns in a freezer-proof container and cover with water. Cover, label and date. Prawns can be frozen for up to 3 months. Thaw in the refrigerator.

For cooked crabs, rock lobsters, bugs and freshwater crayfish, place in an airtight container or cover well with cling film and refrigerate for up to 2 days. If they are green (raw), cover them with a damp cloth or cling film and refrigerate for up to 2 days.

& shellfish

Do not plunge crustaceans straight into boiling water, as doing so will toughen the flesh. The easiest and kindest way is to place live crustaceans inside a plastic bag and place them in a freezer for 1 hour or until they are immobilised. Remove from the plastic bag and immediately plunge into boiling water.

Crustaceans can be frozen raw or cooked. Wrap individually in cling film and place in a freezer bag. Remove all air from the freezer bag and seal. Label and date. Crustaceans can be frozen for up to 3 months. Thaw in the refrigerator.

Scallops on the half shell should be placed in a single layer on a large plate. Cover with a damp cloth or paper towel and refrigerate for up to 24 hours. Scallop meat can be refrigerated for up to 2 days inside an airtight container.

To freeze, place the meat in a freezer proof container or plastic bag. Cover, seal, label and date. Scallop meat can be frozen for up to 3 months. Thaw in the refrigerator.

Oysters on the half shell should be placed in a single layer on a large plate. Cover with a damp cloth or paper towel and refrigerate for up to 24 hours. They can also be frozen on the half shell. Place them on a tray with a few drops of diluted lemon juice. Cover with cling film, label and date. Freeze for up to 3 months. Thaw in the refrigerator.

For mussels, pipis and clams, place in a large bowl and cover with a damp cloth. Refrigerate for up to 24 hours. Mussels, pipis and clams are best frozen without the shells. Remove the meat and place inside a plastic bag

and then a freezer bag. Remove all air from the bag and seal. Label and date. Freeze for up to 3 months. Thaw in the refrigerator.

Clean octopus, cuttlefish and squid thoroughly before storing. Place in an airtight container and refrigerate for up to 2 days. To freeze, wash them thoroughly and wrap in cling film. Place inside a freezer bag, label and date. Freeze for up to 3 months. Thaw in the refrigerator.

With abalone, place the shells in a large bowl and cover with a damp cloth. Fresh abalone will live for 3–5 days in a refrigerator. To freeze it is best to shuck the abalone, wrap them in cling film and place inside a freezer bag. Remove all air and seal. Label and date. Freeze for up to 3 months.

Grilled Skate with Black Bean Sauce & Asian Greens

SERVES 4 AS A MAIN

PREPARATION TIME: 25 minutes

WINE STYLE: medium-dry riesling

1½ tablespoons fermented black beans, rinsed (see page 157)

2 cloves garlic, finely chopped

2 tablespoons light soy sauce

1 teaspoon sugar

80 ml (⅓ cup) grapeseed oil

4 heads bok choy, quartered

4 small skate fillets, skinned and trimmed

extra grapeseed oil

2 spring onions, thinly sliced

Mash the black beans with a fork and combine with the garlic, soy sauce, sugar and grapeseed oil. Mix together thoroughly.

Heat the sauce in a wok over medium heat, add the bok choy and toss for 2 minutes or until tender. Remove the bok choy with a slotted spoon. Reserve the remaining sauce.

Preheat a grill to high. Brush the skate with oil, place on the grill and cook for 2 minutes on each side or until the flesh is golden and fish is just cooked.

Divide the bok choy between 4 serving plates, top with the fish and spoon over a little of the remaining sauce. To serve, garnish with spring onions.

ALTERNATIVES
boneless fillets, gemfish, ling, blue eye, snapper, Atlantic salmon, ocean trout

Grilled Tandoori Ling with Cucumber & Mint Yoghurt

SERVES 4 AS A MAIN
PREPARATION TIME: 40 minutes
WINE STYLE: medium-dry gewurztraminer

MINT YOGHURT
1 large cucumber, peeled and diced
2 tablespoons finely chopped mint
a pinch of white sugar
500 ml (2 cups) plain yoghurt

TANDOORI PASTE
4 cloves garlic, chopped
1 tablespoon grated ginger
2 small tomatoes, chopped
2 teaspoons ground coriander
1 teaspoon turmeric
1 tablespoon white vinegar
125 ml ($\frac{1}{2}$ cup) plain yoghurt
2 teaspoons chilli powder
$\frac{1}{4}$ teaspoon ground fennel
1 tablespoon chopped coriander leaves

4 medium-sized ling fillets
(about 180 g/6 oz each), trimmed
vegetable oil

For the mint yoghurt, combine the cucumber, mint, sugar and yoghurt in a bowl. Cover and refrigerate until ready to use.

For the tandoori paste, place the garlic, ginger, tomatoes, coriander, turmeric, vinegar, yoghurt, chilli powder, fennel and coriander in a food processor and blend until smooth. (Add a little oil if the mixture is too dry.)

Preheat the grill to high.

Coat both sides of the fillets with tandoori paste and cook on the grill for 2–3 minutes on each side or until the fish is just cooked through.

Place the fish on serving plates. Top with a large spoonful of cucumber and mint yoghurt. Serve with steamed basmati rice.

ALTERNATIVES
blue eye, gemfish, boneless fillets, sea perch

Grilled Tuna Steaks with Wasabi & Basil Butter

SERVES 4 AS A MAIN

PREPARATION TIME: 25 minutes

WINE STYLE: medium-bodied pinot noir

WASABI BUTTER

2 teaspoons wasabi paste (see page 160)

2 tablespoons finely chopped basil leaves

1 teaspoon soy sauce

juice of 1 small lime

100 g (3½ oz) unsalted butter, softened

4 medium-sized tuna steaks (about 180 g/6 oz each), trimmed

olive oil

salt and pepper

1 bunch rocket, stems removed

In a small bowl, combine the wasabi, basil, soy sauce, lime juice and butter. Mix together thoroughly and spoon onto a sheet of greaseproof paper (or aluminium foil) and roll into a long cylinder. Wrap tightly and refrigerate until firm.

Preheat the grill to high.

Brush both sides of the tuna with oil and season with salt and pepper.

Place the tuna on a hot grill and cook for 1–2 minutes on each side or until just cooked (tuna can be served slightly raw in the centre).

Remove the butter from the refrigerator and slice into 5 mm (⅛ in) discs.

Place the tuna on serving plates and top with a slice of butter. Serve with rocket.

ALTERNATIVES

swordfish, marlin, skate, boneless fillets, ling

Coconut & Ginger Grilled Mackerel

1 small onion, chopped

2 cloves garlic, chopped

2 small red chillies, seeded and chopped

2 tablespoons grated ginger

1 teaspoon turmeric

a pinch of saffron threads, soaked and drained

2 tablespoons lime juice

80 ml (⅓ cup) coconut milk

3 tablespoons chopped coriander

salt

4 medium-sized mackerel fillets (about 175 g/6 oz each)

lime wedges for serving

Place the onion, garlic, chilli, ginger, turmeric, saffron liquid, lime juice, coconut milk and coriander in a food processor or blender. Blend for about 3 minutes or until a smooth paste is formed. Season to taste with salt, then place in a shallow dish.

Place the fish in a single layer in the coconut mixture and coat both sides evenly. Cover and refrigerate until ready to cook.

Preheat the grill to a medium to high temperature. Place the fillets on the hot grill and cook for 2 minutes on each side, or until just cooked through.

Serve with steamed rice and lime wedges.

ALTERNATIVES
trevally, mullet, morwong, sardines (pilchards), tuna, Atlantic salmon, ling, boneless fillets

Salt-grilled Salmon Skewers with Coriander & Mint Pesto

SERVES 4 AS A STARTER
PREPARATION TIME: 30 minutes
WINE STYLE: unoaked chardonnay

**4 large salmon steaks
(about 200 g/7 oz each), trimmed**

olive oil

sea salt

PESTO

1/2 cup coriander leaves

1/2 cup mint leaves

1/4 cup pinenuts

1 clove garlic

1/2 teaspoon sugar

juice of 1 small lime

125 ml (1/2 cup) olive oil

salt and white pepper

lime wedges to serve

Cut and slice each salmon steak into 2 cm (¾ in) cubes. Thread a bamboo skewer (pre-soak skewers for 5 minutes in warm water) through the fish, using four fish cubes per skewer. Brush with oil and season generously with sea salt. Cover and refrigerate until ready to use.

Preheat the grill to high.

Meanwhile, combine the coriander, mint, pinenuts, garlic, sugar and lime juice in a food processor and process until finely chopped. With the motor running, slowly pour in the oil and process to a smooth paste. Taste and season with salt and pepper.

Place the salmon skewers on the grill and cook for 1–2 minutes. Turn and cook for a further 1–2 minutes or until just cooked.

To serve, arrange the skewers on a large plate with a small bowl of coriander and mint pesto and lime wedges.

ALTERNATIVES
ocean trout, blue eye, ling, tuna, swordfish, marlin

Snapper in Vine Leaves with Tomato & Bocconcini Salad

SERVES 4 AS A MAIN

PREPARATION TIME: 40 minutes

WINE STYLE: cool-climate sauvignon blanc

4 snapper fillets
(about 175 g/6 oz each), trimmed

8 large vine leaves, in brine or fresh,
rinsed (see page 160)

olive oil

2 cloves garlic, chopped

sea salt and cracked black pepper

6 pieces bocconcini, sliced
(see page 157)

4 large ripe tomatoes, sliced

4 tablespoons
finely chopped basil leaves

3 tablespoons olive oil

1 tablespoon balsamic vinegar

Slice each fillet in half crossways. Place each portion of fish on a damp vine leaf. Drizzle with a little olive oil and sprinkle with garlic, sea salt and cracked black pepper. Wrap and secure with a toothpick. Repeat for all portions. Brush the outside of the vine leaves with a little more olive oil.

Preheat the grill or barbecue to high.

Arrange the bocconcini, tomatoes and basil in a bowl and toss together with oil and vinegar. Set aside.

Place the fish on the grill and cook for 2 minutes on each side or until tender to the touch.

Serve immediately with the bocconcini and tomato salad.

ALTERNATIVES
kingfish, trevally, morwong, dory, flathead

105

Peppered Sea Perch with Garlic Potatoes & Parsley Oil

SERVES 4 AS A MAIN
PREPARATION TIME: 35 minutes
WINE STYLE: light-bodied pinot noir

4 medium-sized potatoes, peeled and cubed

2 cloves garlic, finely chopped

olive oil

PARSLEY OIL

½ cup chopped parsley

½ cup chopped basil

1 clove garlic, chopped

250 ml (1 cup) olive oil

salt and pepper

4 medium-sized sea perch fillets (about 200 g/7 oz each), trimmed

cracked black pepper for coating

Preheat the oven to 200°C.

Arrange the potatoes in a shallow baking dish, sprinkle with garlic and drizzle over the olive oil. Bake for 25–30 minutes or until golden.

In a food processor, blend the parsley, basil and garlic until finely chopped. With the motor running, gradually pour in the oil and process until smooth. Season to taste with salt and pepper. Pour into a storage container and set aside.

Preheat the grill to high.

Lightly coat the fillets in olive oil and rub the cracked black pepper all over. Place on the hot grill and cook for 2–3 minutes on each side or until tender to the touch.

To serve, arrange potatoes in the centre of serving plates, top with the fish and drizzle with parsley oil.

ALTERNATIVES
blue eye, ling, ocean perch, Atlantic salmon, gemfish, snapper

Grilled Whole Flounder with Lemon & Thyme

**4 whole flounder
(about 250 g / 8 oz each), cleaned
2 tablespoons butter, melted
2 tablespoons thyme leaves
salt and pepper
2 large lemons, quartered**

Remove the top and bottom fins of the fish with kitchen scissors. Make a small cut at the tail of the fish to remove the skin from the flesh. Place your hand on the tail and gently pull the skin towards the head, moving your hand upwards as the flesh is exposed. Turn the fish over and repeat on the other side.

Preheat the grill to medium-high. Line the grill tray with aluminium foil and brush with a little melted butter. Brush one side of the fish with the remaining butter and sprinkle with thyme. Season with salt and pepper.

Place the buttered flounder on the tray, buttered side up, and slide into the centre rack. Grill for 3 minutes. Carefully turn the fish over, brush with butter and grill for a further 3 minutes or until the fish is opaque and just cooked through. Test with a knife.

Place the fish on serving plates and serve immediately with lemon wedges.

ALTERNATIVES
sea perch, dory, snapper, ocean perch, morwong, garfish,
whiting, pilchards (sardines)

PREPARATION TIME: 20 minutes

WINE STYLE: full-bodied chardonnay

Grilled Lobster
with Salsa Verde

2 medium-sized green (raw) lobsters

SALSA VERDE

2 egg yolks

1 tablespoon lemon juice

1 cup parsley leaves

1 cup basil leaves

½ cup thyme

2 cloves garlic

2 tablespoons capers

250 ml (1 cup) grapeseed oil

sea salt and white pepper

Place the lobsters in the freezer for 1 hour or until they are 'asleep'. Cut in half lengthways and rinse gently under cold running water. Cover and refrigerate until ready to use.

For the salsa verde, place egg yolks, lemon juice, parsley, basil, thyme, garlic and capers in a food processor and process for 1 minute. With the motor running, gradually pour in the oil and process until well combined. Season to taste with salt and pepper. Remove from the food processor and set aside.

Preheat a barbecue or grill to medium heat.

Remove the lobster from the refrigerator and brush the flesh generously with the salsa. When the barbecue or grill is hot, place the lobster on top, shell side down, and cook for 5–6 minutes. Turn the lobster to cook flesh for a further 1–2 minutes, or until the shells have turned bright orange and flesh is just cooked through.

Remove the lobster from the heat and arrange on serving plates. Serve immediately with the remaining salsa verde.

ALTERNATIVES
bugs, prawns, calamari (squid), cuttlefish, mussels

SERVES 4 AS A STARTER
PREPARATION TIME: 20 minutes
WINE STYLE: medium-dry chenin blanc

Grilled Prawn Skewers with Pernod Mayo

PERNOD MAYO
2 large egg yolks
1 tablespoon lemon juice
1 teaspoon Dijon mustard
1 tablespoon Pernod
250 ml (1 cup) vegetable oil

16 large green (raw) king prawns
olive oil for basting

For the Pernod mayo, combine the egg yolks, lemon juice, mustard and Pernod in a food processor and blend. With the motor running, gradually pour in the oil and continue to process until thickened. Pour into a small dipping bowl and refrigerate until ready to use.

Preheat the grill to high.

Devein the prawns, leaving the heads and tails intact.

Thread bamboo skewers through the length of the prawns and brush with olive oil. Place the skewered prawns on the grill and cook for 1–2 minutes on each side or until pink.

To serve, place prawn skewers on a large serving plate with the mayo.

ALTERNATIVE
scallops

SERVES 4 AS A MAIN
PREPARATION TIME: 35 minutes
WINE STYLE: medium-bodied chardonnay

Lime-marinated Bugs

8 medium-sized green
(raw) Balmain bugs

juice of 1 large lemon

juice of 4 medium-sized limes

½ teaspoon lime zest

5 cloves garlic, finely chopped

1 teaspoon sugar

1 small red chilli, finely chopped

1 tablespoon finely chopped dill

½ cup finely chopped parsley

4 tablespoons olive oil

salt and pepper

lime wedges to serve

Slice the bugs in half lengthwise. Rinse gently under cold running water and set aside.

For the marinade, combine the lemon juice, lime juice and zest, garlic, sugar, chilli, dill, parsley and oil. Season to taste with salt and pepper.

Pour the marinade over the bugs, cover and refrigerate for 15–20 minutes.

Preheat the grill or barbecue to high.

Remove the bugs from the marinade and place on the barbecue or chargrill, shell side up. Keep basting with the remaining marinade. Cook for 2–3 minutes on each side or until the shells turn orange and the flesh is just cooked through.

To serve, arrange the bugs on a large platter with lime wedges.

ALTERNATIVES
prawns, crabs, lobsters, freshwater crayfish, scallops, mussels

PREPARATION TIME: 1 hour 15 minutes

WINE STYLE: unoaked chardonnay

Crispy
Barbecued Octopus

125 ml (½ cup) olive oil

3 tablespoons lemon juice

1 clove garlic, chopped

2 tablespoons chopped parsley

2 tablespoons chopped chives

500 g (1 lb) baby octopus, cleaned

In a bowl, combine the olive oil, lemon juice, garlic, parsley and chives. Add the octopus and coat generously with the mixture. Cover and refrigerate for up to 1 hour.

Preheat the grill to high.

Place the octopus on the grill, baste generously with the marinade and cook for about 10 minutes or until crispy.

ALTERNATIVES
calamari (squid), cuttlefish, prawns, crabs, bugs

SERVES 4 AS A STARTER
PREPARATION TIME: 10 minutes
WINE STYLE: full-bodied chardonnay

Oysters Kilpatrick

4 rashers bacon, finely chopped
2 large tomatoes, finely diced
1 tablespoon finely chopped parsley
4 tablespoons Worcestershire sauce
12 large oysters on the half shell
lemon wedges to serve

Preheat the grill to high.

In a bowl, combine the bacon, tomatoes, parsley and Worcestershire sauce. Spoon over the oysters.

Cook under the grill until the bacon is crispy.

Serve with lemon wedges.

ALTERNATIVES
mussels, scallops, bugs, freshwater crayfish (eg yabbies, marron)

Sugarcane Prawns with Dipping Sauce

SERVES 4 AS A STARTER
PREPARATION TIME: 20 minutes
WINE STYLE: dry riesling

1 kg (2 lb) green (raw) banana prawns, peeled and deveined

1 tablespoon fish sauce

¼ cup chopped coriander leaves

2 large egg whites

salt and pepper

12 tinned sugarcane sticks in juice, about 10 cm (4 in) each (see page 160)

2 tablespoons vegetable oil

DIPPING SAUCE

2 tablespoons sugarcane juice

1 tablespoon brown sugar

3 tablespoons fish sauce

1 clove garlic, finely chopped

1 small red chilli, finely chopped

Place the prawns, fish sauce, coriander, egg whites, salt and pepper in a food processor and blend until smooth. Transfer to a bowl.

Using wet hands, mould the prawn paste around one end of each sugarcane stick. Brush lightly with oil.

Preheat the grill to high. Arrange the sugarcane sticks on the grill and cook for about 5 minutes, turning frequently, until the paste is firm to the touch.

For the dipping sauce, combine the sugarcane juice, sugar, fish sauce, garlic and chilli. Place in a small bowl.

To serve, arrange the sugarcane sticks on a large plate and serve with the dipping sauce.

ALTERNATIVES
redfish, blue grenadier, royal red prawns

SERVES 4 AS A MAIN
PREPARATION TIME: 50 minutes
WINE STYLE: cool-climate sauvignon blanc

Sea Perch Fillets with Hot Tomato Broth

**4 large sea perch fillets
(about 175 g/6 oz each),
trimmed and halved**

2 tablespoons olive oil

4 large very ripe tomatoes, peeled

2 cloves garlic, finely chopped

¼ teaspoon cayenne

**a pinch of saffron threads,
soaked in 1 tablespoon water**

**1 litre (4 cups) fish or
chicken stock (see pages 157 & 158)**

salt and pepper

1 small zucchini, finely julienned

Brush the fillets with oil and refrigerate until ready to cook.

Slice the tomatoes in half and remove the seeds by gently pushing through a strainer placed over a saucepan. Discard seeds. Chop the flesh finely and combine with any leftover juices, garlic and cayenne in a saucepan.

Cook the tomato mixture over medium heat for 10 minutes. Remove from the heat and strain the mixture into bowl. When all the liquid has passed through the strainer, return to the saucepan and stir in the saffron. Gradually pour in the stock, season with salt and pepper, and bring to a gentle simmer. Taste and adjust the seasoning.

Meanwhile, season the fillets with salt and pepper and place on a hot grill for 2 minutes on each side, or until just cooked through.

Place the grilled fillets in the centre of shallow serving bowls and ladle over the hot tomato broth. Serve immediately with a sprinkle of julienned zucchini.

ALTERNATIVES
blue eye, ling, boneless fillets, tuna, swordfish, gemfish

Curing & Marinating

Carpaccio of Yellowtail

Scallop Seviche

Gravlax with Dill Mustard Sauce

Swordfish Carpaccio with Orange & Basil Oil

Salad of Raw Tuna with Ginger & Sesame

Sugar-cured Atlantic Salmon

Marinated Sardines with Feta & Olives

Tuna Tartare

Tuna Sashimi with Soy & Wasabi

Pacific Oysters with Sweet Vinaigrette

Prawn & Avocado Wrapped in Nori

Sydney Rock Oysters with Coriander & Lime

Prawn, Mango & Avocado Cocktails

Marinating

MARINATING raw seafood tenderises and adds flavour to the meat, which is eaten raw.

The liquid used for marinating is usually uncooked and contains an acid base, oil and a selection of herbs and spices. Avoid using salt, as this draws out the moisture from the food.

Marinating with a strong acid marinade can 'cook' the seafood.

Equipment

A glass, enamel or ceramic dish.

Stainless-steel mixing bowl or container (never aluminium, iron or copper).

How to marinate raw seafood

The raw seafood used must be very fresh and of excellent quality. Seafood pieces should be quite small or sliced very thinly.

Prepare a marinade of your choice. Place the seafood in the container and pour over the prepared marinade.

Cover and place in a cool place, preferably the refrigerator. (Flavours mature faster at room temperature, but so does bacterial growth!)

Marinating for longer than 4 hours will firm the flesh and reduce the fresh flavours of seafood.

CURING seafood means coating the seafood in salt and sometimes sugar to preserve the seafood. This process draws out the moisture from seafood and in turn produces a brine.

One benefit of curing with salt and sugar is that it inhibits bacterial growth.

Equipment

A glass, enamel or ceramic dish.

Stainless steel mixing bowl or container (never aluminium, iron or copper).

Cling film or plastic wrap.

How to cure

Place cleaned and filleted seafood in a single layer in a container. Sprinkle generously with salt and/or sugar. Turn over and repeat for the other side. Place another layer on top and repeat the process.

Cover the salted seafood and refrigerate for at least 1 hour for each 500 g (1 lb) fillet.

When ready to serve, wipe the salt and/or sugar mixture from the seafood using a clean, damp cloth or rinse carefully under cold running water.

Curing

Carpaccio of Yellowtail

1 teaspoon lemon zest

juice of 1 large lemon

salt and white pepper

½ teaspoon sugar

4 tablespoons grapeseed oil

1 tablespoon light soy sauce

1 teaspoon finely chopped parsley

250 g (8 oz) yellowtail fillets, cleaned and skinned

1 tablespoon finely chopped chives

Combine the zest and half the lemon juice in a mixing bowl. Whisk in the salt, pepper, sugar, oil, soy sauce and parsley. Taste and add the remaining lemon juice if necessary. Set aside for 10 minutes.

Slice the yellowtail fillets diagonally into paper-thin slices.

To serve, arrange the slices of yellowtail on serving plates, drizzle over a little of the dressing and sprinkle with chives.

ALTERNATIVES
pilchards (sardines), whiting, garfish, tuna, swordfish, Atlantic salmon, ocean trout

Scallop Seviche

800 g (1½ lb) scallops, roe removed

juice of 4 large limes

juice of 1 large lemon

1 clove garlic, finely chopped

1 large sweet red chilli,
seeded and chopped

⅓ cup finely chopped coriander

1 large tomato, finely diced

salt and pepper

1 large avocado

Cut the scallop into a small dice. Cover and set aside.

Combine the lime and lemon juices, garlic, chilli, coriander, tomato, salt and pepper. Add the scallops and toss together gently. Cover and refrigerate for up to 1 hour.

Peel and remove the stone from the avocado. Chop into a small dice and toss gently into the scallop mixture. Serve immediately on chilled serving plates.

ALTERNATIVES
oysters, mussels, sea perch fillets, ling, whiting

SERVES 6 AS A STARTER
PREPARATION TIME: 25 minutes
WINE STYLE: medium-bodied chardonnay

Gravlax with Dill Mustard Sauce

1 very fresh Atlantic salmon fillet (about 600–800 g/1–1½ lb), skin on

2 tablespoons sea salt

2 tablespoons sugar

½ cup chopped fresh dill

2 tablespoons white peppercorns, crushed

lemon wedges to serve

DILL MUSTARD SAUCE
125 ml (½ cup) sweet mustard
125 ml (½ cup) sour cream
¼ cup chopped fresh dill
1 tablespoon lemon juice
salt and pepper

Using tweezers, carefully remove any pin bones from the salmon. Slice the salmon in half lengthways and trim both pieces to the same size and shape.

Combine the sea salt, sugar, dill and white peppercorns. Sprinkle an even layer of the curing mixture over the base of a deep glass dish. Place half the salmon, skin side down, on the curing mixture. Sprinkle generously with some of the curing mixture and cover with remaining salmon fillet, skin side up. Sprinkle over the remaining curing mixture. Cover tightly with cling film and refrigerate overnight or for up to 24 hours.

For the dill mustard sauce, combine the sweet mustard, sour cream, dill, lemon juice, salt and pepper. Cover and refrigerate until ready to use.

Remove the fillets from the dish and wipe with a clean damp cloth. Slice the salmon thinly on the diagonal, down towards the skin, in the direction of the tail.

Serve on a large plate with the dill mustard sauce and lemon wedges.

ALTERNATIVES
ocean trout, tuna

SERVES 4 AS A STARTER

PREPARATION TIME: 15 minutes

WINE STYLE: unoaked semillon

Swordfish Carpaccio with Orange & Basil Oil

2 tablespoons finely chopped orange zest

100 ml (3½ fl oz) olive oil

2 tablespoons finely chopped basil leaves

sea salt and cracked black pepper to taste

450 g (14½ oz) swordfish fillet

Combine the orange zest, oil and basil in a bowl. Season with salt and pepper and mix together thoroughly. Cover and refrigerate until ready to use.

Slice the fish on the diagonal into paper-thin slices. Arrange on a large plate, overlapping each slice.

Drizzle over the orange and basil oil and serve immediately.

ALTERNATIVES

tuna, Atlantic salmon, ocean trout

Salad of Raw Tuna
with Ginger & Sesame

250 g (8 oz) sashimi-grade tuna

a pinch each of salt and white pepper

½ teaspoon sesame oil

½ tablespoon soy sauce

½ tablespoon mirin (see page 159)

½ teaspoon minced ginger

½ teaspoon minced garlic

2 large mint leaves, finely chopped

1 tablespoon
finely chopped basil leaves

1 large egg yolk

1 tablespoon sesame seeds

1 cup small rocket leaves

Cut the tuna into small dice and place in a mixing bowl.
Season with salt and pepper. Set aside.

In another bowl combine the sesame oil, soy sauce, mirin, ginger,
garlic, mint and basil. Pour the sauce over the tuna and toss together gently.
Add the egg yolk and sesame seeds and combine gently.

To serve, place the tuna on serving plates in small mounds and garnish
with rocket leaves.

ALTERNATIVES
Atlantic salmon, garfish, ocean trout, whiting, scallops, oysters, cuttlefish

SERVES 6 AS A STARTER
PREPARATION TIME: 25 minutes
WINE STYLE: medium-bodied chardonnay

Sugar-cured Atlantic Salmon

1 very fresh salmon fillet (500–600 g/1 lb), skin on

4 tablespoons white caster sugar

2 tablespoons sea salt

2 tablespoons finely chopped tarragon leaves

60 ml (¼ cup) olive oil

cracked black pepper

Place the fillet on a flat, dry surface and remove any bones with a pair of tweezers. Slice in half lengthways and trim both pieces to the same size and shape.

In a bowl, combine the sugar, salt and tarragon. Take a sheet of plastic wrap twice the length of the salmon fillet. Sprinkle half the curing mixture into the centre of one half of the cling film. Place the fillet, skin side down, on the sugar mixture. Sprinkle the sugar mixture on the fish and cover with the remaining fillet, skin side up. Sprinkle with the remaining sugar mixture. Fold the plastic wrap over the fish and secure tightly. Place a plate or board on top of the fish to weight it down. Refrigerate overnight or for up to 24 hours, turning the fish after 12 hours.

Remove the salmon fillet from the cling film and wipe the remaining sugar mixture from the fish with a clean damp cloth.

Slice the salmon diagonally into thin slices, down towards the skin, in the direction of the tail. Arrange each slice, slightly overlapping, on a large plate.

Drizzle with olive oil and season with pepper. Serve with thinly sliced toasted bread.

ALTERNATIVES
ocean trout, whiting, ling, dory, flounder

SERVES 4 AS A STARTER
PREPARATION TIME: 20 minutes
WINE STYLE: lightly oaked marsanne

Marinated Sardines with Feta & Olives

20 sardine fillets
125 ml (½ cup) white wine vinegar
2 teaspoons sea salt
2 cloves garlic, finely chopped
⅓ cup finely chopped parsley
100 ml (3½ fl oz) olive oil
1 small red chilli, seeded, finely chopped
150 g (5 oz) Bulgarian feta
1 large Spanish onion, finely sliced
10 large green olives, pitted and finely sliced

Gently wash and pat dry the sardines. Cut into strips and place in a shallow non-metallic bowl.

Combine the vinegar, sea salt, garlic and half the parsley. Pour over the sardines, cover and refrigerate for 3–4 hours.

Combine the olive oil, chilli and remaining parsley. Cover and set aside until ready to use.

Drain the vinegar mixture from the sardines. Pour the oil mixture on, and gently toss to coat the sardines thoroughly. Cover and refrigerate until ready to use.

To serve, crumble the feta and place in the centre of a large serving plate. Arrange the sardine fillets around the feta and sprinkle with the onions and olives.

ALTERNATIVES
whiting, Atlantic salmon, ocean trout, rainbow trout, garfish

Tuna Tartare

500 g (1 lb) very fresh tuna fillet

2 spring onions, finely chopped

2 tablespoons capers,
rinsed and chopped

2 tablespoons finely chopped parsley

125 ml ($\frac{1}{2}$ cup)
crème fraîche or sour cream

6 medium-sized kalamata olives,
seeded and finely chopped

2 tablespoons lemon juice

sea salt and cracked black pepper

1 medium-sized cucumber,
peeled and julienned

lemon wedges to serve

Finely dice the tuna and place in a glass bowl. Add the spring onions, capers, parsley, crème fraîche (or sour cream), olives and lemon juice. Gently toss together and season to taste with salt and pepper. Cover and refrigerate until ready to use.

Divide the tuna mixture into four portions and pile each portion into the centre of chilled serving plates. Top with julienned cucumber and sprinkle with cracked black pepper. Serve with lemon wedges.

ALTERNATIVES
Atlantic salmon, ocean trout, swordfish

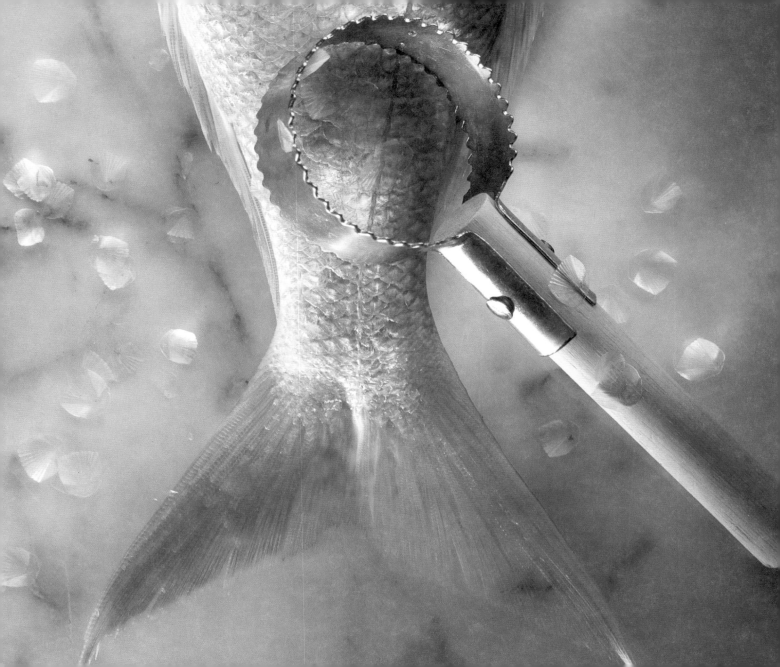

SERVES 4 AS A STARTER
PREPARATION TIME: 15 minutes
WINE STYLE: unoaked chardonnay

Tuna Sashimi
with Soy & Wasabi

400 g (14 oz) sashimi-grade tuna
2 teaspoons wasabi powder
1 tablespoon mirin (see page 159)
125 ml (½ cup) soy sauce

Cut the tuna into thin slices.

Combine the wasabi powder with the mirin to make a paste.
Stir into the soy sauce and place in a small dipping bowl.

Place the tuna on a large serving plate with the dipping sauce.
Serve with chopsticks.

ALTERNATIVES
swordfish, Atlantic salmon, ocean trout, cuttlefish, garfish,
trevally, oysters

SERVES 4 AS A STARTER
PREPARATION TIME: 15 minutes
WINE STYLE: dry riesling

Pacific Oysters
with Sweet Vinaigrette

6 tablespoons grapeseed oil
2 tablespoons white wine vinegar
1 clove garlic, finely chopped
1 small tomato, finely chopped
2 tablespoons finely chopped chives
1 tablespoon finely chopped basil
a pinch of sugar
12 large oysters on the half shell

Combine the oil, vinegar, garlic, tomato, chives, basil and sugar in a bowl and whisk together thoroughly. Cover and refrigerate until ready to use.

To serve, spoon the vinaigrette over the oysters and serve immediately.

ALTERNATIVES
mussels, prawns, scallops, bugs, fresh crabmeat, freshwater crayfish, lobsters

Prawn & Avocado Wrapped in Nori

SERVES 4 AS A STARTER

PREPARATION TIME: 25 minutes

WINE STYLE: sauvignon blanc

4 tablespoons whole egg mayonnaise
(see page 160)

1 teaspoon wasabi paste
(see page 160)

6 nori sheets, halved

2 cups steamed short-grain rice

12 king prawns,
cooked, shelled and deveined

2 large avocados, peeled and sliced

2 cucumbers, cut into 5 cm (2 in) lengths

soy sauce

Combine the mayonnaise and wasabi paste in a small bowl, mix well and set aside.

Lay the nori sheets on a flat, dry surface, rough side up. Place a spoonful of steamed rice on the left half. Flatten the rice and spoon over a little of the mayonnaise mixture. Top with prawns, avocado slices and cucumber. Roll into the shape of a cone. Repeat with the remaining ingredients.

Serve with soy sauce for dipping.

ALTERNATIVES
fresh crabmeat, scallops, smoked salmon, oysters, mussels

Sydney Rock Oysters with Coriander & Lime

60 ml (¼ cup) olive oil

3 tablespoons lime juice

2 tablespoons finely chopped coriander

1 tablespoon finely chopped chives

1 teaspoon soy sauce

1 teaspoon sugar

cracked black pepper

16 large rock oysters, shucked

Combine the oil, lime juice, coriander, chives, soy sauce and sugar in a mixing bowl. Stir in the pepper to taste. Cover and refrigerate until ready to use.

Spoon the sauce over the oysters and serve immediately.

ALTERNATIVES
mussels, scallops, prawns, bugs

Prawn, Mango & Avocado Cocktails

SERVES 4 AS A STARTER
PREPARATION TIME: 15 minutes
WINE STYLE: unoaked semillon

1 kg (2 lb) cooked school prawns, shelled and deveined
2 large avocados, diced
2 large mangoes, diced
2 large tomatoes, diced
3 tablespoons balsamic vinegar
3 tablespoons olive oil
3 tablespoons chopped coriander
1 bunch watercress

In a mixing bowl, carefully toss together all the ingredients except the watercress. Divide salad between four serving plates.

To serve, garnish with watercress.

ALTERNATIVES
crabmeat, scallops, mussels, lobsters, bugs,
freshwater crayfish (eg yabbies and marron)

Simmering

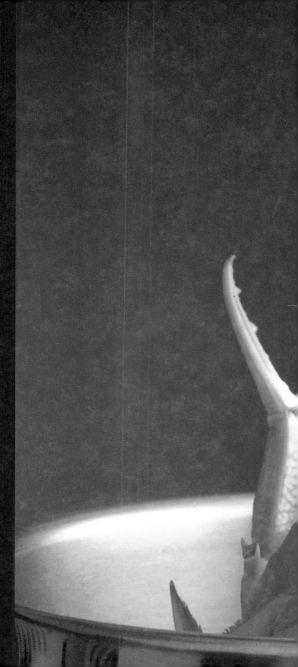

Laksa

Red Mullet Soup

Coconut Curry of Leatherjacket

Fish Dumplings in Lime & Chilli Broth

Octopus Stewed in Red Wine

Scallop & Prawn Ravioli with Fresh Tarragon

Oysters & Shiitake Mushrooms in Miso Broth

Bouillabaisse

Seafood Paella

Clam Chowder

Cockle Risotto

Hot & Sour Prawn Soup

Lobster Soup

Saffron Fish Stew

Tiger Prawn Bisque

Simmering

Equipment

Any large, deep cooking pot that will hold the seafood with sufficient liquid.

How to simmer

Seafood can be simmered in lightly salted water, court-bouillon or any suitable stock.

Prepare enough liquid to cover the seafood completely. (As a guide, the liquid should be four times the volume of the seafood.) Place the seafood into boiling liquid, bring back to the boil then reduce to a simmer and cook, covered, for the desired length of time. Drain immediately.

SIMMERING involves cooking seafood in a liquid, usually water or stock. It occurs just below boiling point, at between 95°C and 98°C.

Simmering is the preferred method for cooking fish because of its soft-textured flesh – fish has tiny connective tissue, and boiling it often causes the flesh to break up.

Simmering is also a quick and convenient way to cook shellfish.

Take care not to overcook crustaceans, as the flesh will become tough and rubbery. When cooked, the shells will turn a shade of orange-red and the flesh will be just firm. Prawns are cooked when the shell turns a shade of pink and the tail has curled under slightly.

SERVES 4 AS A MAIN

PREPARATION TIME: 45 minutes

WINE STYLE: medium-bodied shiraz

Laksa

200 g (7 oz) dried rice vermicelli noodles

1 tablespoon oil

4 tablespoons laksa paste
(see page 158)

1.5 litres (3 pints) fish stock
(see page 158)

500 ml (2 cups) coconut milk

1 teaspoon sugar

4 kaffir lime leaves, shredded
(see page 158)

500 g (1 lb) ling fillets,
cut into large chunks

1 cup bean sprouts

2 small fresh red chillies, finely chopped

1/3 cup coriander leaves

Bring a saucepan of water to the boil. Add the noodles and cook for 2–3 minutes. Drain well and set aside.

Heat the oil in a large saucepan or wok over medium to high heat. Add the laksa paste and sauté until fragrant, about 3 minutes.

Add the fish stock and bring to the boil. Reduce the heat and add the coconut milk, sugar and lime leaves. Allow to simmer for 8–10 minutes.

Add the fish and simmer for a further 2 minutes, or until the fish is tender.

Divide the noodles between four bowls. Add some bean sprouts to each bowl and ladle in the soup. Garnish with chilli and coriander leaves. Serve immediately.

ALTERNATIVES

blue eye, boneless fillets, morwong, ocean perch, gemfish

Red Mullet Soup

4 medium-sized red mullet
(about 150 g/5 oz each)*

salt and white pepper

1 tablespoon olive oil

1 small onion, chopped

1 stalk celery, chopped

1 medium-sized fennel bulb, chopped

2 cloves garlic, sliced

4 small tomatoes, chopped

1 teaspoon Pernod (optional)

1 litre (4 cups) fish stock (see page 158)

1 teaspoon saffron threads,
soaked in a little water

2 tablespoons finely chopped chives

* ask your fishmonger to fillet,
reserving heads and bones

Season the fillets with salt and pepper. Cover with plastic wrap and refrigerate until ready to use.

Heat the oil in a large saucepan over medium heat, add the fish bones and cook for 5–6 minutes. Add the onion, celery, fennel, garlic and tomatoes and cook for a further 5 minutes. Stir in the Pernod and combine well. Pour in the fish stock and saffron and slowly bring to the boil. Reduce to a medium heat, season with salt and pepper. Gently simmer for 15–20 minutes.

Pass the contents of the saucepan through a fine-meshed sieve into another saucepan and return to a low heat. Taste and adjust the seasoning.

Heat the oil in a frying pan over medium heat, add the fillets and cook, skin-side down, for 1–2 minutes. Gently turn the fillets over and cook for a further minute, or until just cooked.

To serve, place the fillets into shallow bowls. Ladle over the hot soup and garnish with chives.

ALTERNATIVES
ocean perch, snapper, blue eye, ling, flathead, morwong

Coconut Curry of Leatherjacket

4 medium-sized leatherjackets, whole, cleaned and skinned

salt and pepper

2 tablespoons vegetable oil

3 tablespoons green curry paste (see page 158)

1 teaspoon ground turmeric

2 small tomatoes, peeled and diced

375 ml (2½ cups) coconut milk

2 tablespoons fish sauce

1 tablespoon lime juice

⅓ cup coriander leaves

lime wedges

Remove tail and fins from the leatherjackets. Season with salt and pepper and set aside.

Heat oil in a large frying pan over medium heat. Add the fish to the pan and cook for 1 minute on each side. Remove and set aside.

Add the curry paste and turmeric to the frying pan and sauté for 1 minute. Add the tomatoes and continue to sauté for a further 4–5 minutes, or until the tomatoes have softened. Add the coconut milk, fish sauce, lime juice and coriander. Simmer for 3–4 minutes. Add the fish and simmer for a further 2–3 minutes, or until the fish is just cooked.

Serve immediately with steamed rice and lime wedges.

ALTERNATIVES

mullet, trevally, Spanish mackerel, tuna, swordfish

Fish Dumplings in Lime & Chilli Broth

250 g (8 oz) fresh thin egg noodles

500 g (1 lb) redfish fillets

½ cup chopped coriander

juice of 1 large lime

1 tablespoon cornflour

1 tablespoon fish sauce

salt and pepper

1 litre (4 cups) fish stock
(see page 158)

4 kaffir lime leaves
(see page 158)

3 small red chillies,
seeded and chopped

1 tablespoon finely grated ginger

Place noodles in a bowl and pour some boiling water over them. Allow to stand for 3–4 minutes. Drain thoroughly and set aside.

Chop the fillets into a small dice and place in a mixing bowl. Add half the coriander, lime juice, cornflour and fish sauce. Season with salt and pepper. Combine until a sticky mixture is formed. With wet hands, shape the mixture into small balls and transfer to a plate. Cover and refrigerate until ready to use.

Heat the stock in a saucepan, add the lime leaves, half the chilli and the ginger and slowly bring to the boil. Drop the dumplings into the boiling stock for about 2 minutes or until they turn opaque. Remove with a slotted spoon.

Divide the noodles between four warmed bowls and top with the fish dumplings. Ladle the hot stock on top and garnish with the remaining coriander and chilli.

ALTERNATIVES
trevally, mullet, boneless fillets, morwong

SERVES 4 AS A STARTER

PREPARATION TIME: 1 hour 45 minutes

WINE STYLE: dry rosé

Octopus Stewed in Red Wine

250 ml (1 cup) olive oil

1 onion, chopped

1/3 cup chopped parsley

750 ml (3 cups) red wine

2 cloves garlic, chopped

1 teaspoon sugar

salt and pepper

750 g (1½ lb) baby octopus

Place the oil, onion, parsley, red wine, garlic, sugar, salt and pepper and octopus in a large saucepan. Simmer gently for 30–40 minutes, stirring every 5–10 minutes. When the juices begin to caramelise, cut a small piece of octopus and check for tenderness. If the octopus is a little tough, add some water and continue to stew for a further 20–30 minutes, or until the octopus is very tender.

Serve warm.

ALTERNATIVES
calamari (squid), cuttlefish

SERVES 4 AS A MAIN
PREPARATION TIME: 40 minutes
WINE STYLE: medium-bodied chardonnay

Scallop & Prawn Ravioli with Fresh Tarragon

12 large scallops, cleaned

12 large green (raw) king prawns, shelled and deveined

2 teaspoons finely chopped tarragon

1 tablespoon finely chopped chives

1 egg white

250 ml (1 cup) cream

salt and pepper

24 wonton wrappers

250 ml (1 cup) fish or vegetable stock (see pages 158 & 160)

2 tablespoons dry white wine

Cut the scallops and prawns into small pieces and combine with the tarragon, chives, egg white, half the cream, and salt and pepper. Mix together thoroughly. Cover and refrigerate for 10–15 minutes, or until ready to use.

Lay a wonton skin on a flat, dry surface. Place spoonfuls of filling in the centre. Dip your finger into a little milk and run it around the edges. Top with another wrapper and press firmly around the edges to seal. Aim to make 3 or 4 ravioli per person.

To make the sauce, place the fish stock, the remaining cream and the white wine in a saucepan and simmer until reduced by half.

Meanwhile, bring a large saucepan of salted water to the boil. Add the ravioli and cook for 4–5 minutes. Drain.

Place the ravioli on serving plates, spoon over the sauce and sprinkle with cracked pepper.

ALTERNATIVES
boneless fillets, bugs, fresh crabmeat

Oysters & Shiitake Mushrooms in Miso Broth

SERVES 4 AS A STARTER
PREPARATION TIME: 35 minutes
WINE STYLE: unoaked chardonnay

20 small rock oysters, shucked

1.5 litres (3 pints) water

6 cm (2½ in) piece konbu (dried seaweed, see page 158)

1 cup dried bonito flakes

3 tablespoons white miso paste (see page 159)

4 medium-sized fresh shiitake mushrooms, finely sliced (see page 160)

1 tablespoon chopped chives

cracked black pepper

Remove the oysters from the shells, reserving all the juices. Strain into a bowl through a fine-meshed sieve and set aside.

Place the water and konbu in a saucepan and slowly bring to a simmer. Then remove the konbu and add the bonito flakes. Slowly bring to the boil. Once the liquid begins to boil, remove from the heat and set aside for 4–5 minutes. Strain through a fine-meshed sieve.

Place the strained liquid into a saucepan. Stir in the miso and reserved oyster liquid. Add the mushrooms and simmer over medium heat for 5 minutes. Add the oysters and remove from the heat instantly.

To serve, ladle the soup into small, deep bowls. Sprinkle with chives and cracked black pepper.

ALTERNATIVES
mussels, clams, pipis, scallops, prawns, abalone

Bouillabaisse

SERVES 4 AS A MAIN

PREPARATION TIME: 30 minutes

WINE STYLE: full-bodied, dry rosé

3 tablespoons olive oil

1 large onion, chopped

2 cloves garlic, finely chopped

2 medium-sized tomatoes, chopped

1 tablespoon tomato paste

1.5 litres (3 pints) fish stock (see page 158)

1 tablespoon chopped basil

60 ml (¼ cup) lemon juice

1 teaspoon chopped thyme leaves

a pinch of saffron threads, soaked in 1 tablespoon water

a pinch of cayenne

1 teaspoon sugar

salt and pepper

500 g (1 lb) ling fillets, cut into chunks

500 g (1 lb) mussels, scrubbed and beards removed

8 large green (raw) prawns, shelled and deveined

Heat the oil in a large, heavy-based pot over medium heat. Add the onion and garlic and sauté until golden. Add the tomatoes and tomato paste and cook for a further 1–2 minutes. Add the fish stock, basil, lemon juice, thyme, saffron, cayenne and sugar. Gently bring the soup to the boil. Season to taste with salt and pepper.

Add the fish, mussels and prawns and simmer for 5–6 minutes, or until the fish and prawns have turned opaque and the mussels have opened. Discard any mussels that have not opened.

Serve immediately in deep bowls with crusty bread.

ALTERNATIVES
boneless fillets, crabs, bugs, clams, pipis, freshwater crayfish

Seafood Paella

60 ml (¼ cup) olive oil

1 large onion, finely chopped

1 medium-sized
red capsicum, cut into strips

3 cloves garlic, finely chopped

2 medium-sized tomatoes,
peeled and chopped

1½ cups short-grain rice

1 litre (4 cups) fish stock (see page 158)

1 teaspoon saffron threads,
soaked in a little water

salt and pepper

2 medium-sized green
(raw) blue swimmer crabs,
cleaned and segmented

500 g (1 lb) ling fillets, cut into chunks

500 g (1 lb) green (raw)
king prawns, peeled and deveined

250 g (8 oz) squid, cut into strips

250 g (8 oz) mussels,
scrubbed and beards removed

⅓ cup chopped parsley

Heat the oil in a large, heavy-based saucepan or wok over medium heat. Add the onion, capsicum and garlic and cook until tender, about 2 minutes. Add the tomatoes and sauté until softened.

Add the rice and coat well with the tomato mixture. Stir in half the stock and cook until partially absorbed. Add saffron liquid, salt and pepper. Add the crabs and pour in the remaining stock a little at a time. Simmer until the rice has absorbed all of the liquid.

Add the remaining seafood, cover and cook for a further 5 minutes or until the mussels have opened and the fish is tender. Discard any mussels that have not opened.

To serve, place paella in a large serving bowl and sprinkle with parsley.

ALTERNATIVES
bugs, clams, pipis, boneless fillets, blue eye, calamari (squid),
freshwater crayfish (eg yabbies and marron)

Clam Chowder

2 tablespoons butter

1 large onion, finely chopped

4 rashers bacon, finely chopped

2 stalks celery, finely chopped

**1.25 litres (5 cups)
fish stock (see page 158)**

1 teaspoon chopped thyme

1 bay leaf

**1 x 440 g (14 oz) tin of
peeled tomatoes, chopped**

2 tablespoons chopped parsley

**2 medium-sized potatoes,
peeled and diced**

salt and pepper

1 kg (2 lb) clams

Melt the butter in a large saucepan over medium heat. Add the onions, bacon and celery and cook until softened. Add the fish stock, thyme, bay leaf, tomatoes, parsley, potatoes, salt and pepper. Simmer for 30 minutes, or until the potatoes are tender.

Meanwhile, scrub the clams and place them in a large saucepan with 250 ml (1 cup) water. Cover and steam until the shells open. Remove and set aside. Discard any clams that have not opened. Remove the meat from the shells.

Taste the soup and adjust the seasoning. Add the clams and simmer for a further minute.

To serve, ladle soup into individual bowls and serve immediately with crusty bread.

ALTERNATIVES
prawns, lobsters, freshwater crayfish, scallops

SERVES 4 AS A MAIN
PREPARATION TIME: 45 minutes
WINE STYLE: full-bodied chardonnay

Cockle Risotto

1 kg (2 lb) cockles, scrubbed
500 ml (2 cups) dry white wine
1 litre (4 cups) fish stock (see page 158)
4 tablespoons butter
1 medium-sized onion, finely chopped
2 cups Arborio rice (see page 156)
2 tablespoons finely chopped parsley
salt and pepper

Place the cockles and white wine in a large saucepan. Steam over medium heat until the shells have opened. Discard any that do not open. Remove the meat from the shells and set aside. Strain the liquid through a sieve lined with a fine cloth to remove any sand. Reserve the liquid.

Place the fish stock in a saucepan and bring to a slow simmer.

In a heavy-based saucepan, melt 2 tablespoons of the butter over medium heat. Add the onion and cook until softened. Add the rice and stir for 1 minute or until the rice is well coated.

Pour in half of the cockle liquid and continue to stir until absorbed. Add the remainder and continue stirring until absorbed. Add the fish stock to the rice, 250 ml (1 cup) at a time, until the liquid is all absorbed. At this point the rice should have a creamy consistency. If more liquid is required, add extra heated stock or water.

When the rice is almost cooked, stir in the remaining 2 tablespoons of butter, the parsley and the reserved clams. To serve, sprinkle with sea salt and cracked black pepper.

ALTERNATIVES
mussels, calamari (squid), cuttlefish, prawns, pipis, clams

SERVES 4 AS A STARTER

PREPARATION TIME: 40 minutes

WINE STYLE: medium-dry riesling

Hot & Sour Prawn Soup

1 kg (2 lb) green (raw) prawns

1 tablespoon vegetable oil

1.25 litres (2 pints) fish or chicken stock (see pages 157 & 158)

3 stalks lemongrass, crushed and sliced (white part only)

6 kaffir lime leaves (see page 158)

2 tablespoons fish sauce

1 tablespoon red chilli paste (see page 159)

3 spring onions, sliced

juice of 2 large limes

2 small red chillies, finely sliced

2 small tomatoes, peeled and diced

6 small mushrooms, halved

1 cup coriander leaves

Shell and devein the prawns. Wash the prawn heads, tails and shells and drain.

Heat the oil in large saucepan over medium heat, toss in the prawn shells and sauté until they turn pink. Pour in the stock and bring to the boil. Add the lemongrass, lime leaves, fish sauce and chilli paste. Reduce the heat and simmer for 10 minutes.

Strain the stock through a fine-meshed sieve and return to the boil. Add the spring onions, lime juice, chillies, tomatoes, mushrooms, prawns and half of the coriander leaves. Simmer for 3–4 minutes or until the prawns turn pink and are just cooked.

To serve, ladle the soup into deep bowls and sprinkle with the remaining coriander leaves. Serve with steamed rice.

ALTERNATIVES
crab, abalone, bugs

Lobster Soup

2 small live lobsters

1 tablespoon olive oil

1 medium-sized onion, finely chopped

1 large carrot, chopped

2 stalks celery, chopped

1/2 cup chopped parsley

2 x 440 g (14 1/2 oz) tins of Italian peeled tomatoes, chopped

1.5 litres (3 pints) water

salt and pepper

125 ml (1/2 cup) thickened cream

Place the lobsters in the freezer for 1 hour or until the lobsters are 'asleep'. Remove from the freezer and slice in half lengthways. Remove all the meat and reserve the shells. Slice the meat into 8 pieces and place in a bowl. Cover and refrigerate until ready to use.

Heat the oil in a large stockpot over medium heat. Add the onion, carrot, celery and lobster shells. Cook for 4–5 minutes, breaking up the lobster shells with a wooden spoon. Add the parsley and tomatoes, stirring constantly. Add the water, cover and simmer for 1 1/2 hours.

Remove the lobster shells and pass the remaining contents through a food mill or sieve, a little at a time, into another stockpot. Place the soup over medium heat and season with salt and pepper. Slowly bring the soup to a boil. Add the cream and reserved lobster meat. Cook for 3–4 minutes or until the lobster is just cooked and no longer translucent. To serve, ladle the soup into individual bowls and garnish with freshly ground black pepper.

ALTERNATIVES
freshwater crayfish, prawns, bugs, crabs

SERVES 4 AS A MAIN
PREPARATION TIME: 1 hour
WINE STYLE: full-bodied, dry rosé

Saffron Fish Stew

3 tablespoons olive oil

4 small shallots, finely chopped

3 cloves garlic, finely chopped

4 medium-sized potatoes,
cut into small dice

4 medium-sized tomatoes, chopped

500 ml (2 cups) fish stock (see page 158)

250 ml (1 cup) white wine

a large pinch of saffron threads,
soaked in a little water

a pinch of cayenne

2 tablespoons chopped parsley

1 tablespoon chopped thyme leaves

4 mulloway fillets (about 150 g/5 oz each),
cut into small chunks

salt and pepper

lemon wedges

Preheat the oven to 170°C.

Place the oil, shallots, garlic, potatoes and tomatoes in a large, heavy-based casserole dish. Add the stock and white wine, followed by the saffron, cayenne, parsley, thyme and fish. Season with salt and pepper and stir together gently.

Cover the casserole with a tight-fitting lid and place in the oven. Cook for 20 minutes, then remove from the oven and stir gently. Cover and return to the oven and cook for a further 10–15 minutes, or until the potatoes and fish are tender.

Remove from the oven and stir gently. Taste and adjust the seasoning.

To serve, ladle the stew into deep bowls and serve with lemon wedges and crusty bread.

ALTERNATIVES

ling, blue eye, boneless fillets, barramundi, gemfish

SERVES 4 AS A STARTER

PREPARATION TIME: 25 minutes

WINE STYLE: sauvignon blanc

Tiger Prawn Bisque

1.5 kg (3 lb) green (raw) tiger prawns

2 tablespoons butter

1 small onion, chopped

4 small tomatoes, chopped

3 tablespoons chopped tarragon leaves

1.5 litres (3 pints) fish stock (see page 158)

salt and pepper

250 ml (1 cup) thickened cream

Peel and devein the prawns, reserving the heads and shells. Refrigerate the prawns until ready to use.

Place the shells in a food processor and process for 30 seconds. Heat the butter in a saucepan over medium heat and cook the onions until softened. Add the shells, tomatoes, half of the tarragon and fish stock. Cover and simmer for 15–20 minutes. Remove from the heat and strain through a fine-meshed sieve.

Return the liquid to the heat and season with salt and pepper. Pour in the cream and stir thoroughly. Add prawns and cook until the prawns turn pink and are no longer translucent. Taste and adjust the seasoning if necessary.

Sprinkle with the remaining tarragon and serve immediately.

ALTERNATIVES
crabs, bugs, scallops, clams, pipis

Glossary

ANGELHAIR PASTA

Angelhair pasta is thin, fine spaghetti. It can easily be replaced with spaghettini, regular spaghetti or linguine. Available from most delicatessens and supermarkets.

ARBORIO RICE

Originally from Italy and now grown in Australia, Arborio rice is a short-grain rice used specifically for risotto. Available from most delicatessens and supermarkets.

BALSAMIC VINEGAR

Balsamic vinegar is made from grape juice aged in wooden barrels over many years. It is dark brown in colour and has a pungent sweetness. Use sparingly. Available from most delicatessens and supermarkets.

BLACK SESAME SEEDS

Sesame seeds are native to India and come in shades of black and brown, but pale cream or white seeds are more common. Black seeds can be substituted for white sesame seeds. Available at Asian grocers and supermarkets.

BOCCONCINI

Bocconcini are small balls of fresh mozzarella packed in water or whey. Available from most delicatessens and supermarkets.

BOK CHOY

Bok choy is also referred to as Chinese cabbage. Both leaves and stems can be used in cooking and are ideal for stir-fries and soups. Available from Asian grocers and supermarkets.

BUCKWHEAT

Buckwheat is a seed native to Russia that is used to make buckwheat flour. It adds a nutty flavour and texture if used in rice dishes and stuffings. Available from most delicatessens and supermarkets.

CHICKEN STOCK

(makes about 2 litres/8 cups)
1.5 kg (3 lb) chicken bones
2 large onions, sliced
2 small carrots, sliced
2 stalks celery, chopped
3 stalks parsley
2 sprigs thyme
1 bay leaf
8 black peppercorns

Place all the ingredients in a large stockpot or saucepan. Cover with cold water and slowly bring to a gentle simmer. Simmer for 3½–4 hours; skim the surface of the stock while simmering. Strain through a fine-meshed sieve and allow to cool.

Refrigerate for 2–3 days or freeze for up to 3 months.

CRÈME FRAÎCHE

Crème fraîche is a mixture of sour cream and fresh cream, and has a slightly sour or tangy flavour. It can be replaced with sour cream. Ideal for sauces and soups, it is available from most delicatessens and supermarkets.

DAIKON

Daikon is a large Japanese radish with a sweet, fresh flavour. It can be used grated in salads or finely shredded as a garnish. Available from good fruit markets.

FERMENTED BLACK BEANS

Fermented black beans, also known as Chinese black beans, are made from small black soy beans preserved in salt. They have a pungent and salty flavour and are usually chopped finely before being added to dishes. Available from Asian grocers and some supermarkets.

FISH SAUCE

Fish sauce is also known as nam pla or nuoc mam and is used as a condiment. Made from salted fish or shrimp, it has a salty flavour. Available from Asian grocers and some supermarkets.

FISH STOCK

(makes about 2 litres / 8 cups)
1 kg (2 lb) fish bones
1 tablespoon olive oil
1 small onion, finely chopped
1 small leek, chopped
1 stalk celery, chopped
2 stalks parsley
2 bay leaves
2 sprigs thyme
8 black peppercorns
250 ml (1 cup) dry white wine

Wash the fish bones thoroughly and chop them into large pieces. Drain well.

Heat the oil in a large stockpot or saucepan over medium heat. Add the fish bones and cook for 3–4 minutes. Add the remaining ingredients, and stir to combine.

Cover the bones with water and slowly bring to a simmer. Simmer for 15–20 minutes. Skim the surface of the stock while simmering.

Strain the stock through a fine-meshed sieve and allow to cool.

Refrigerate for 1–2 days or freeze for up to 2 months.

GREEN CURRY PASTE

A hot and spicy paste made from fresh green chillies, blended with aromatic herbs and spices. Available from Asian grocers and most supermarkets.

HALOUMI

Haloumi is a stringy and salty cheese made from goat's milk. Haloumi can be cut into slices and grilled or fried in a little oil. Available from good delicatessens and supermarkets.

HOKKIEN NOODLES

Hokkien noodles are fresh yellow egg noodles. Commonly used in Chinese cooking, they are ideal for stir-fry cooking and can be served hot or cold. Available from Asian grocers and some supermarkets.

HORSERADISH

Horseradish is a white, spicy root. Fresh horseradish is available from good fruit markets and preserved in jars from supermarkets.

KAFFIR LIME LEAVES

The fragrant leaves from the kaffir lime tree are essential in Thai cooking. Available fresh from all good fruit markets.

KONBU

Konbu is dried kelp used to make dashi (Japanese soup stock). When using konbu, wipe the surface gently with a damp cloth. Washing konbu will remove the flavour. Store for up to six months in a cool, dry place. Available in long sheets or smaller pieces from Asian supermarkets.

LAKSA PASTE

Laksa paste is a blend of ingredients usually including chillies, onions, garlic, ginger and oil. Available from Asian grocers and delicatessens.

MIRIN

Also known as Japanese rice wine, mirin is a sweet-flavoured liquid made from steamed glutinous rice and alcohol. Available from Asian grocers and the gourmet section of some supermarkets.

MISO PASTE

Miso is a fermented paste made from soy beans. Red miso paste is made from barley and soy beans, whereas white miso is made from rice and soy beans. Usually prepared as miso soup, this Japanese staple is highly nutritious. Available from Asian grocers.

PINK PEPPERCORNS

Pink peppercorns are not really peppercorns but berries from the Baies rose plant. These berries have a pungent, sweet flavour and are usually found packed in brine or water. Available from good delicatessens and supermarkets.

RED CHILLI PASTE

Red chilli paste is a hot sauce made from fresh red chillies combined with other ingredients such as onion, garlic and vinegar. Also known as sambal oelek, it is available from Asian grocers and most supermarkets.

RED CURRY PASTE

A hot and spicy paste made from ground red chillies, aromatic herbs and spices. Available in glass jars from Asian grocers and most supermarkets.

RICE PAPER

Rice paper is a thin, translucent paper made from rice flour, water and salt. Available in dry form in various sizes. Rice paper needs to be soaked in warm water briefly before being used as a wrapping. Available from Asian supermarkets.

SAFFRON

Saffron comes from the dried stigmas of the purple crocus flower. The world's most expensive spice, it takes up to 200 000 stigmas to produce one kilogram of saffron. Commonly used in paella, bouillabaisse and risotto. Available in threads (whole stigmas) or in powder form from delicatessens and good supermarkets.

SAKE

Sake is a Japanese wine made from fermented rice. Used for both cooking and drinking, sake should be kept tightly sealed in the refrigerator. Available from liquor stores and Asian supermarkets.

SANSHO PEPPER

Sansho is an aromatic Japanese pepper made from the berries of the prickly ash tree. Sansho is usually bought ground and is closely related to the Chinese Sichuan pepper. Available from Asian supermarkets.

SHIITAKE MUSHROOMS

The shiitake mushroom was first cultivated in Japan and Korea. The caps of these mushrooms are dark brown, with a pale cream underside. The meaty flesh has a distinctive 'steak-like' flavour. The stems tend to be a little tough, but are ideal to use in stocks. Available fresh from good fruit and vegetable stores. Dried shiitake mushrooms should be soaked in warm water for at least 30 minutes.

SOBA NOODLES

Soba noodles are Japanese noodles made from buckwheat and wheat flour. Great in soups or served cold. Available from Asian supermarkets.

SUGARCANE STICKS

Sugarcane sticks are available fresh or packed in syrup. To use as a snack or garnish, peel the light brown skin away from the flesh and cut into strips. Available from Asian grocers.

TOASTING NUTS

Toasting nuts brings out their flavour. Toast them in a frying pan over medium to high heat for 3–4 minutes, or in the oven in an oven tray for up to 6–7 minutes. Shake the pan frequently to toast evenly. Toast until golden brown.

VINE LEAVES

Large green leaves from the grapevine are commonly used in Greek and Middle Eastern cooking. Vine leaves can be used as a wrapping or a garnish. Available fresh and packed in brine from most delicatessens and supermarkets.

WASABI PASTE

Wasabi is Japanese horseradish and comes from the root of the Japanese plant, *wasabi japonica*. Available in powder or paste form from Asian supermarkets.

WHOLE EGG MAYONNAISE

A rich, American-style mayonnaise made from whole eggs. Available from good delicatessens and supermarkets.

VEGETABLE STOCK

(makes about 3 litres)
2 large onions, chopped
4 cloves garlic, peeled
3 tablespoons olive oil
2 leeks, chopped
2 large carrots, chopped
3 stalks celery, chopped
1 small bunch mixed fresh herbs
  (eg basil, parsley, thyme)
bay leaves
black peppercorns
4 litres water

Place all ingredients in a large stockpot or saucepan. Cover with cold water and slowly bring to a gentle simmer. Simmer for 2½–3 hours. Skim the surface of the stock while simmering.

Strain through a fine-meshed sieve and allow to cool. Refrigerate for 2–3 days or freeze for up to 6 months.

Index